Advance praise for *Forget Perfect*

"An utterly disarming, congenial, and self-effacing book of charming workaday wisdom about being a woman in the real world."

> —Ruth Campbell Williams, author of *Younger Than That Now: A Passage from the Sixties*

"*Forget Perfect* should be given to every person at graduation and at marriage and at first big job, at first child, and again at midlife crisis! It's a book to be read again and again. There are a lot of self-help books that are inspiring, empowering and enlightening. *Forget Perfect* is all those . . . plus one more vital asset . . . It's ennobling!"

> —Chip R. Bell, author of *Managers as Mentors*

"Need a 'get out of jail card' for your perfectionism? Read *Forget Perfect* and find the power and beauty in a different way to live your life."

> —Julie Anixter, managing director, tompeterscompany!

"Lisa's message really hit home with me; it gave me a new perspective and I never laughed so hard in my life."

> —Lyné Brown, director of sales, Clorox Corporation

"Our staff and our parents loved it. *Forget Perfect* has become our new mantra."

> —Mary Anne Charron, middle school principal

"It's easy to get caught up in the details with work and the kids. Lisa helped me step back and think about what was really important to me."

> —Emily A. Graffeo, senior manager, Daimler Chrysler

"This was just what I needed. This book helped me realize that I was so busy trying to do absolutely everything, I had forgotten how to enjoy it."

—Carol Carson, PTA president and
self-professed "super-woman"

"Most of these gurus talk a good game—it sounds great when you read it but it never goes much further. Lisa goes beyond just talking, she gets people to actually do it."

—Durwood Snead, president, CMD Group

"Lisa Earle McLeod speaks from experiences common to us all. Girls and women of all ages will find much wisdom here. Lisa skips right over self-pity, focusing instead on the humor inherent in every woman's desire to make all the people in her life happy all of the time."

—Patricia Crone, director, Atlanta Girls School

FORGET PERFECT

Finding joy, meaning,
and satisfaction in the life
you've already got and the
you you already are

LISA EARLE MCLEOD
with JoAnn Swan Neely

A Perigee Book

A Perigee Book
Published by The Berkley Publishing Group
A division of Penguin Putnam Inc.
375 Hudson Street
New York, New York 10014

First edition: November 2001

Published simultaneously in Canada.

Visit our website at www.penguinputnam.com

Library of Congress Cataloging-in-Publication Data

Earle, Lisa.
    Forget perfect / Lisa Earle McLeod with
JoAnn Swan Neely.
        p.   cm.
    ISBN 0-399-52715-X
    1. Self-actualization (Psychology)
    2. Women—Psychology.
    I. Swan, JoAnne.   II. Title.

BF637.S4 E36 2001
158.1'082—dc21
                                    00-068473

PRINTED IN THE UNITED STATES OF AMERICA

10   9   8   7   6   5

In honor of

Frances Bell Earle 1939–1992

Teacher, mother, activist, and I hope at our next meeting, friend

and

Pearl Bates Swan 1915–1997

Who did her best even when things were at their worst

CONTENTS

ACKNOWLEDGMENTS

No novice writes a book without a lot of support from her family and friends. I am indeed fortunate to have such a great "committee" on my side. I would like to thank them for their unique and wonderful contributions. My family:

My husband, Bob, for believing his crazy wife could do anything she set her mind to and reminding her of it whenever she needed it. I'm forever grateful that you're the one I ran into.

My two amazing daughters—Elizabeth, for being a thoughtful and generous spirit who helped me listen to my voice, and is the model of a great writer, and Alex, for cheering me up with the afternoon office danceathon and just by being your sparkling self.

My father, Jay Earle, for giving me the gift of gab and the tenacity to see it through.

My stepmother, Judy, for sharing her life stories with me and shamelessly giving out copies as only a proud mother knows how.

Leslie, for providing the Xer perspective and patiently teaching her pathetic older sister that it's not just a big typewriter.

Jim—not too many brothers would take the time to read

and provide insightful commentary on a women's self-help book, and his wife, Sherri, for helping out on a few technical terms.

The original editorial advisory board whose early and endless support I couldn't have lived without:

Steve Fugate, the prototype for the great guy, whose humor and creativity inspired the quizzes, not to mention the title. To his wife, Deb, for sharing her thoughts on small-town life and the gracious tolerance she shows her husband's chatty friend.

Ann Wapstra, your willingness to laugh at yourself and shining example of what real friendship is all about are inspirational. And yes, you are a very wise woman indeed.

Judith Wheeler, whose painstaking proofreading kept my poor editing skills a secret until they couldn't back out.

The two incredible professionals that turned a talker into a writer: My agent, Laurie Harper, a sales and literary goddess on whose every word I hang. Your fortitude, foresight, and friendship made all the difference in the world. I knew I loved you the first time I read your bio. My brilliant editor, Sheila Curry Oakes, whose attention to detail and commitment to her craft improved my material immensely. May you be eternally rewarded for the patience and stamina you displayed in steering a rookie through the process.

All the rest of the committee members:

Chip Bell, who enthusiastically mentored a novice.

Gail Cangiano, for rescuing me from Laurie's slush pile.

Carol Carson, for her help and expertise on my marketing materials.

Pat Fields, for providing the inspiration for the wise woman.

Shannon Foster, the giver of JIT feedback; I'm upping the ante on the next one.

Emily A. Graffeo, who willingly shared her "intro" perspective of the world.

Myra Hellmund, for describing her experiences and giving me commentary on the installment plan.

Juanita Boyles Neely, whose enthusiastic proofreading caught the last few before it was too late.

Jennie Noonan, for taking the time to provide candid and correct feedback when I needed it.

Jodie and Mark Mesler, for rereading their silly neighbor's book every time she changed two words.

Larry Lowenstein and his book publishing class for some much needed instruction. Those two pushy women who monopolized all the discussions had a plan after all.

Jane Moore, for putting a new face on breast cancer for me.

Marieke and Magda, for keeping the kids at bay while I cranked it out.

Debby Richmond, who loved it from the start.

Scott Ross, for producing my videos and giving me the starving artist rate.

Kenny and Nathan Simmons, your reaction to that letter gave me more confidence than you can imagine.

Teressa Tanner, the Wal-Mart moment was priceless.

Ellen Marion Velcoff, a great and supportive friend with wonderful taste in holiday gifts.

Tove Pedersen White, a true history friend.

Bobbie Williams, I learned more sitting in on your first grade writing workshop than the entire time I was in college.

And everyone else who shared their thoughts, stories, and ideas with me: Angie, Allison, Barbara, Bettye, Bonnie, Carol D., Donna, Elaine, Emily, Frankie, Frankie Lynn, Gladys, Gail, Holly, Jan, Karen, Laura, Melita, Micki, Nancy S., Nancy T., Rachelle, Lyné, Lynn, Tracy, and all those women who found themselves opening up to that nosy lady next to you on an airplane. Now you know why she was taking notes while you spilled your guts.

Two women who only the most frazzled of proofreaders could miss: Cindy Dean, a great and funny pal and the most well-traveled woman I know; and Meg Hartin, a delightful friend who took the time to provide thoughtful feedback and early support.

The folks who worked on the logistical side: Terri Hennessey for all her help; the team at Putnam for their creative and marketing support; Joan Perrin-Falquet for her beautiful cover art; Mary Beavers for getting a halfway decent picture of me; Chris Houser and Jon Geganto for putting together my Web site; and the ladies at the Five Forks branch of the Gwinnett Public Library for helping me with the research, and Kat Caverly of Katakismet Design for putting together a great-looking marketing package.

A special thanks to Mark and John Neely, for sharing your wife and mom for two years.

And lastly, I am eternally grateful to my wonderful friend and partner, JoAnn Swan Neely. Your support as we shared this journey will never be forgotten. We did it!

OH, WHAT A DIFFERENCE SHE MADE

Every woman at some point in her life has a "moment." It's that instance in time where you quit going through the motions and actually think about your life and what it all really means. I've heard some people describe these as "aha" moments. When I think of aha moments I imagine someone standing on the top of a mountain with a clear view of the universe below, and in that moment the meaning of life becomes clear to them.

Most of my friends and I have had the more typical moment that comes from too much work, no sleep, twenty unreturned voice mails, a lack of clean underwear, and a few unpaid bills that culminates in a "What the hell am I doing with my life?" crying jag. Rather than refer to these as nervous breakdowns, which is what they feel like, I will call them a "flash." The basis for this book is some of the conclusions we've reached during our own personal flashes as we tried to ponder the "What the hell am I doing with my life?" question.

My biggest flash occurred at my mother's funeral when I

was twenty-nine years old and seven months pregnant. My mother had died at the age of fifty-three after a yearlong battle with breast cancer. We hadn't had one of those "she's my best friend" relationships that seem to exist only in feminine hygiene ads. In fact, we had several fallings-out over the years, but during her illness we were able to put that behind us and become close again. Cancer does that.

Here I was at her funeral. I had on my very expensive maternity suit and looked quite the sophisticate. I was the embodiment of my mother's dream, a professional woman about to have my first child, proof that women really could have it all.

After a few of the usual words from the priest, he turned it over to several people who had asked to speak. First, one of her students spoke about how my mother had encouraged his love for science. Then, a note was read from another student about how my mother helped her through teen alcoholism. She wrote about how my mother had recognized her problems and had gotten her and her family into counseling. One of our neighbors spoke about how Mom had challenged the developers of a major highway and forced them to put in nature trails as part of the project. She had rallied all of the neighbors to her cause and ten years later those trails are still being enjoyed daily.

As the list went on and on, I started wondering if I was at the right funeral! Was this the same woman who lost it on a daily basis, screaming while her children ignored her, the poor housekeeper who got orange shag carpet in the '70s and kept it until the '90s because it hid stains, the same woman who thought cut-up SPAM on top of baked beans counted as a casserole? Surely this was not the woman being so eloquently eulogized. Sure, I knew she was a teacher and had been in charge of some citizen's group, but wasn't she really just my mother, after all?

Over the years, I had questioned how good she was at that. We had not been close and there were times I was sure I hated her. Yet here we were, her three children sitting in the front row, each of us a success in our own right. Other neighborhood kids had taken a wrong turn here or there. Looking at the other families I grew up with I realized that there was at least one screwup in every family. But not those Earle children, they were all on their way, without a bad one among us. We all assumed that it was our own doing, but I had just realized the common denominator.

In addition to us, there were two foster children that she took in for three years before they were placed for adoption. One was now in college and the other one about to start. Their adoptive mother spoke lovingly about the time they spent with our family and how much my mother had helped them. It was, she said, "a turning point in their lives."

My father summed up the service when he said, "In the words of that old country song, you left the woodpile higher than you found it."

As I watched these people pay tribute to my mother I thought long and hard about what a difference she had made in these lives. As a teacher, community activist, neighbor, wife, foster mother, and, of course, as my mother. She wasn't perfect, far from it, yet she had obviously played a major role in the lives of everyone there. All of the people that spoke sighted her influence as *significant*.

I started to wonder, what would my funeral be like? What would people say? I was sure I had surpassed my mother in terms of accomplishments. Certainly I had done more with my life than she had by twenty-nine. I was making a great living. I was the best salesperson in the history of my company, money being, of course, the measurement tool. I had a beautiful home, a successful marriage, I was expecting a baby, and I would soon be back at work managing it all looking like a Virginia Slims ad.

As I ticked off my many proud accomplishments I was again haunted by the thought, "But what will they say?" Who would be the person to stand up and talk about how I helped them at the turning point in their life? My customers? Well I was a great sales rep, but let's be realistic: I sold training programs, not polio vaccines. My neighbors? My yard did look pretty good these days and I'm sure they all appreciated the fact that I researched historic paint palettes before I chose my color scheme. Who else?

My friends? Well, come to think of it how many real friends did I have? I gave a great Christmas party every year, but how many of those people was I really important to? Was everyone in my life just an acquaintance?

There I was the consummate professional, perfectly groomed,

the embodiment of all my mother's dreams for me, proof that the hard work she put into the Women's Movement really paid off; yet, the sum of my accomplishments to date seemed to be that I contributed 15 percent to my 401K, had a standing appointment with my hairdresser to touch up my roots, and ate a low-fat diet.

It was pretty depressing. Where were the people to make the glowing tributes about the major impact I had had on their lives? At this point I was wondering who, if anyone, would even come, much less have something to say. Maybe I needed an angel like Clarence in *It's a Wonderful Life*, to show me my impact, but I didn't see anyone who would stand up and say, "Oh what a difference she made to me."

That was the flash, the moment when I realized that things weren't right. I didn't know quite what was wrong. I had done everything I was supposed to; but it just wasn't right. That brief moment of insight was where this book began. It wasn't a book at first, it was a flash, a "What the hell am I doing with my life?" moment that happened in the front row of the Robert J. Murphy Funeral Home in Arlington, Virginia. It evolved into a book when I realized I wasn't the only one floundering.

Most of us have to go through some major tragedy to realize what matters to us. I hope I can give you that perspective without your having to suffer. I want you to figure out *now* what takes most of us a few deaths, children, and other assorted life-altering events to figure out. One of our goals when JoAnn and I began this project was to give each woman a ten-year jump in perspective. Things are always clearer in hindsight and I want to give you a "frontsight" that is just as clear.

One of the other things I hope you get out of this book is a greater appreciation for yourself and other women. You're probably already doing more than you know, but you don't have anyone to point it out to you.

As I've thought of my mother's funeral and how surprised I was at the scope of her influence, I realize that she too would have been quite shocked by the service. To her, life probably seemed like an endless to-do list that she could never seem to get checked off. I doubt that she ever saw how much she meant to people because she never felt close enough to them to ask. I wonder if she was ever really even happy.

We all wish that we could go back in time to people we've lost and make things different. If I could reenter my mother's life I wouldn't go back as her daughter. I would go back as someone else—a friend. That's what I suspect she and a lot of other women really need. Don't you deserve someone to remind you of all the wonderful life choices you've already made, to point out to you how much you have meant to people, to help you figure out where *you* want to go from here? Everyone needs that wonderful person who doesn't want or need anything from us who listens unbiasedly and helps us find our inner voice.

As I think about that funeral, and everyone saying what a difference my mother made to them, I can see what a difference a friend like that could have made to her; she needed a Clarence.

Well, I can't go back in time and do it for her, so I'm going to try to do it for you. I'm hoping I can be that friend for you and help you become that friend for yourself and others.

Why Me?

Whether the other women you'll meet in this book and I have our own lives together is questionable depending on what day you ask us. We're not organized, never get around to writing thank-you notes, and I for one consider Tuna Helper a staple of my family's diet, but more about these personal failings later. That's why this book is not about how to help you become a more perfect anything. Let's leave that to Martha, Dr. Spock, *Good Housekeeping*, and those other people we like to hold up as personal standards of everything we're not.

A friend of mine said, "Every time I look at a self-help book, I already feel tired and behind." Well, honey, this is the book for you. There are no queens of perfect here. I don't want to show you how to do more, get better organized, rise through the ranks of corporate America, or plan your menus a week in advance; the rest of us have tried all that and frankly it left us feeling rather flat.

I'm tired of people setting some impossible standard for us; that's why most of my suggestions involve doing LESS, not more. This isn't six steps to change your life or a yearlong self-improvement plan. It's a story—a story about what really matters to women and how what really matters to you is probably in the life you've already got.

You deserve to find some joy and happiness in your life—the life you're living now and what's yet to come. You deserve to feel significant, to know that no matter what you're doing with it, your life does count. I want you to live your life knowing that at your funeral everybody will be saying, "Oh what a difference she made to me."

FORGET
PERFECT

CHAPTER ONE

Is This It?

"I feel like I'm not doing a good enough job of anything. I'm not being a good enough mother, I'm not doing everything I should be at work, and I'm not being a nice enough wife. Everywhere I turn, I'm letting someone down."

—Kristine, age thirty-six,
marketing executive and mother of two toddlers

PICTURE PERFECT

When I was younger I always had a picture of what life was going to be like when I grew up. My picture involved business travel because for some reason this represented the pinnacle of success to me. If you were so important they couldn't live without your brilliance in another city you must really be somebody, right?

If you're thinking, what is this woman talking about? I never dreamed of a career. All I wanted was motherhood, martyrdom, or whatever—you can fill in the blank. If you stop and think for a minute, I bet you too had some picture in your mind of how perfect things where going to be when you grew up. Try to remember that picture and read on.

Here's what my picture looked like: jetting from one place to another, carrying an expensive briefcase, wearing designer suits; I would have my own assistant, breeze in and out of important meetings, make the big bucks, and a Helen Reddy song would play as the soundtrack to my exciting life.

Well, by the time I was twenty-nine that's exactly what I was doing, more or less. But I felt like my theme song was "Workin' in a Coal Mine." Where was the thrill? Where was the glamour? Where was Helen?

As far as exciting travel goes, I remember one incident that seemed to sum it all up. My cab squealed into the airport with just enough time to check my bag and make my flight. As I threw my bag and a buck at the skycap, he barked, "What city?" My mind went blank. I knew my flight was at 6:30, but all of a sudden I realized I didn't have any idea where I was going. Not only that, I didn't even know where I was at the time. I actually had to check my ticket to figure it out. My exciting career had become a blur of airports, cabs, offices, and hotel rooms.

Oh, I *looked* the picture all right, but wasn't it supposed to feel different from this? What bothered me even more than the sheer physical drain of it all was the lack of significance. I had thought I would feel really important, I had thought I would make a difference . . . I had thought . . . I would be happy.

Shortly after the airport incident, I decided to find out if the rest of the feminine world was handling grown-uphood any better. My totally unscientific research consisted of late-night telephone talks with my friends, completely unprofessional conversations with customers, and a random sampling of women I met on airplanes.

I started with a little quiz. Take it yourself and see how you fare. No one's going to check your answers, so be honest.

When I was a little girl dreaming about growing up, I hoped my life would:

A. Include a lot of really difficult, hard work so that I could practice handling high-stress situations on four hours of sleep.

B. Feel so out of control most of the time I couldn't even remember what I originally had in mind.

C. Have a fair share of problems that would enable me to demonstrate my strength and perseverance.

D. Be at least a little better than my mother's,

When I look back on those little-girl dreams, I think that:

A. It's amazing how each and every one came true exactly the way I hoped it would.

B. Those motivational posters in the school guidance office really worked.

C. It's surprising that I could make such an accurate assessment of the way the world works at such a young age.

D. I must have been living in La-La Land.

The way my life really turned out is:

A. Toiling merrily away in my home with the white picket fence, where my clean and polite children skip happily out to greet Daddy when he comes up the walk at 5 o'clock.

B. Days of bon-bons and nights of caviar ever since I was swept off my feet by a fabulously handsome and fabulously wealthy man who lives to make me smile.

C. A high-powered world where all major decisions are made by me and carried out by a stream of underlings eager to do my bidding.

D. Nothing close to the above, just an average existence that includes some of the same daily frustrations as everyone else's.

My current relationship with my partner:

A. Is a soul-mate connection that fills my every emotional want and need.

B. Has a burning-hot passion that smolders when we're apart and ignites every time we even look at each other.

C. Seems like a one big nonstop date filled with unlimited fun, laughter, and romance.

D. Is pretty mundane most of the time, except when we're in a fight.

My work is:

A. A whirlwind of excitement and thrills that I would do even if I wasn't paid the handsome salary I am.

B. The fulfillment of a lifelong dream and better than I had ever hoped.

C. A way to make a lasting contribution to humanity and one that fills me with a sense of purpose every minute of the day.

D. Something I fell into, and keep doing because it pays the bills and I don't have the time or energy to think of anything else.

Most of the people I see in and around my community:

A. Make a special effort to go out of their way to make me feel welcome everywhere I go.

B. Work hard alongside me to achieve our shared vision of life.

C. Care very deeply about me and my family.

D. Can't remember my last name.

I think spending all day, every day, with young children can be:

A. So exciting, because you never know what those darlings will do next.

B. A relaxing way to pass the time.

C. An excellent avenue for my creative problem-solving skills.

D. A little bit harder and lonelier than I thought it would be.

In general, I find that men are:

A. My intellectual and emotional equals with whom I have a lot in common.

B. Acutely aware of others' moods and feelings, and eager to talk about them.

C. Always noticing things around the house that need doing and then doing them.

D. Necessary at times.

I'm saving my best outfit for:

A. The next Inaugural Ball where I plan to dance the cha-cha with the new commander-in-chief.

B. My *Today Show* interview when I am proclaimed home-maker of the year.

C. The day I am invited to speak at the Harvard commence-ment.

D. What the heck am I saving that thing for, this is as good as my life gets!

When I think of my home, I think of it as a:

A. Haven and refuge away from the outside world.

B. Bold design statement that reflects who I am.

C. Showplace for graciously entertaining my many friends.

D. Big, fat mess that always needs work.

My friends are people I:

A. Talk with on a daily basis about the meaning of life.

B. Go to wild parties and dance all night with.

C. Have known most of my life and are available to assist me in any endeavor.

D. Vaguely remember and hope to see again really soon.

My personal financial situation is:

A. The result of a well-thought-out plan I have been diligently following for many years.

B. Providing me with a life of leisure and luxury.

C. An important cornerstone of my life that I monitor daily, giving it the time, attention, and energy it deserves.

D. Something I'd rather not think about.

Most nights when I go to bed, I:

A. Know that I've done a good day's work and others appreciate my efforts.

B. Take pleasure in reliving the many wonderful moments of my day.

C. Compose poetry to soothe my soul.

D. Fall asleep with the television on.

As I look back on the last few years I:

A. Feel 100 percent confident that I've made all the right choices and wouldn't change a thing.

B. Am so very glad everything didn't go right for me, because I've so enjoyed all these "growth opportunities."

C. Have that serene sense of calm that comes from knowing I've fulfilled my destiny as a woman.

D. Wonder where in the heck all that time went.

If other people took a close look at my life they would see:

A. A calm and gentle soul, serene and content because she knows that it's both an honor and a privilege to be the rudder of her family.

B. A self-assured hard charger who lives by the seat of her pants, high on adrenaline and a lust for life.

C. A carefree spirit, able to indulge her every fantasy, pleasure, and whim on a moment's notice.

D. A woman so frazzled she drove five miles past her exit before she even realized it.

The phrase that best describes me is:

A. Earth Mother, goddess of nature.

B. Commander of the Universe, ruler of all.

C. Princess of the Palace, pampered and petted.

D. Very tired.

If most of your answers were D, you are: NORMAL

If most of your answers were A, B, or C, you are: ANNOYING

Put this book down immediately and begin working on world peace because you are the only person I know that has it together. You obviously never watched television as a child and therefore had completely realistic expectations about what life would hold for you. And these expectations are now being utterly fulfilled by your hard work, intelligence, and can-do attitude. Rah, rah, you!

As for everyone else, well, read on a bit and see if some of this stuff helps you feel better about the life you're leading or perhaps arrange things a little differently from now on. I hope reading this book will help you to lighten up on yourself, once you realize that no one else's life is really perfect either.

IT'S PROBABLY JUST ME

You're still reading, so my guess is you must have had a few Ds on your list, just like every other woman I've ever met. Oh, and that woman who exudes the self-satisfied glow of someone who makes all the right choices? Well, I never ran into her, except maybe in a menopause ad.

Interested to know what some real women had to say about their lives? Well, for starters, I wasn't the only one a little disillusioned about this whole work nonsense:

"Who are these women that 'have it all?' I don't know where they find the time. It's all I can do to keep my head above water at work. My husband and I both travel so we haven't gotten our schedules together to conceive a child, much less raise one. This really isn't turning out the way I thought it would."

—Donna, vice president of a major healthcare company

"All my life I knew I was supposed to be a teacher. Everyone in my family always said I'd be great at it. Now after ten years in the classroom, I just hate it. I can't believe I'm thinking of quitting. How will I tell my parents? They were always so proud of their daughter, the teacher."

—Amanda, a disgruntled teacher from North Dakota

Here I thought I was making this major contribution for the last two years, and now that I've been promoted, I find out that my old position isn't even going to be replaced, because it's 'non-essential to our core mission.' Thanks a lot. I wish somebody had told me that when I was working all those weekends. What exactly do we do around here?"

—Tracy, a big-time manager for a Fortune 500 company

The report from the domestic front isn't a whole lot rosier:

"You would think I'd have more time for myself, since I'm home, but I can't even remember the last time I read the paper. I've heard about 'ladies who lunch' but I can't even get myself organized enough to call a friend and arrange it, much less go."

> —Jan, a stay-at-home mother of two, who says her new career is chauffer

"I always wanted to be part of a close, happy family since I never had one growing up. That's what I thought I was getting when I married into this bunch. Close, tell me about it. My mother-in-law is so close to us I feel like I'm suffocating. If that woman starts one more conversation with 'Whatcha need to do is . . .', I will not be responsible for my actions."

> —Marilyn, on living near her in-laws

"That's my whole life, taking care of other people. I handle all the details to make everyone else's life run smoothly. Well, who's my backup person? I graduated summa cum laude and I'm embarrassed to fill out my form for the alumni directory because I have to put housewife on it. I'm not married to the house."

> —Ellen, after leaving a megabucks sales job to stay home with her kids

"You set up all these great rules for the baby-sitter about no TV or videos, then within a half an hour of my being home with them I find myself asking if they want to watch something. Now was this the kind of mother I was waiting all those years to be?"

—Ann, an executive who finally became a mother at age forty-five by adopting two children

"All I ever wanted was to have kids, but I never dreamed they would take so much out of me. Maybe I'm an awful mother or something, but whenever the agency offers a trip, I don't even care if it's to Timbuktu, I take it just to get a break."

—Cindy, part-time travel agent and mother of two

"I guess I should have another baby now that my first is going off to school. I mean, how else can I call myself a stay-at-home mom when nobody's home?"

—Allison, a stay-at-home mother of an only child who's going off to kindergarten

"The cashier at the grocery store asked for my work number the other day and I went into this big, long explanation of how I used to work and will probably go back and now I'm at home and I'm OK with it and I really do a lot and I don't watch soaps, and blah, blah, blah. All this, for a seventeen-year-old that didn't know what a kumquat was."

—Shannon, after deciding to stay home with her kids

As for the men in our lives? Well, as any friend of mine will tell you, they're certainly not helping the situation:

"A date, forget it. If anyone actually asked me on one, I'm not sure I would understand the question. Besides I'm too tired after work for another round of 'Oh my, that sounds like such an interesting job, tell me more about it.' A pet is looking better all the time."

—Suzanne, on still being single at forty-two, and tired of being asked why

"I don't know where I got this idea that marriage would be so great. This is my second try and I'm beginning to think I wasn't cut out for this."

—Adrian, contemplating divorce number two

"I thought that when I got married I had a best friend for life, but now I wonder if we even know each other. I guess it's like they say; we're from two different planets. Did anyone actually prove that there was intelligent life on Mars?"

—Janice, after being married for twenty-five years

JoAnn summed it all up pretty well after her mother's funeral when she said,

"I realized that I could die tomorrow and I would never have had any fun. That's all I've ever done is work. Work at home, work at work, work with my son, just plain work!!!"

I don't want to give you the impression that everyone I know lives a wretched hell of an existence. Quite a number of them had some good things to say about kids, jobs, husbands, and the lot. And a few of them even reminded me of those annoying women you see in magazines that talk about how they use some great time-management system and organize their medicines alphabetically. But over and over again, I heard, "I'm doing everything I was supposed to do, so why isn't my life everything I thought it would be?"

At this point, it should be pretty obvious—it's not just you. And here's the good part—not only is it not just you . . .

It's not your fault!

I'm no shrink, but something must be wrong if *every single one of us* is convinced that somewhere, somebody else out there is managing it better. Her life must be bliss, right? We don't know her, but we're sure she's out there. Well, she's not. And you know what I think is wrong with the rest of us? I think we've been sold a bill of goods on this whole "perfect" thing. The world has us convinced that being perfect and doing more are the keys to a great life. Somewhere along the line, we bought into the notion that all the happiness and good things in life are reserved for the perfect people and until we become one of them, all our problems are our own damn fault!

Surely any unhappiness we're experiencing stems from the fact that we aren't organized, don't read enough, aren't good enough mothers, don't work hard enough, eat too much refined sugar, don't exhibit good enough listening skills, or whatever the hell else was in this month's *Cosmo* quiz.

And then, as if we don't make things bad enough by comparing ourselves to the most perfect people we can find, there's an entire industry of books, tapes, and whatnot out there highlighting every possible aspect of our inadequacies. Combine that with unsolicited advice from strangers and your own relatives (don't get me going on families) and it's a wonder any of us have the strength to face another day as our oh-so-*un*perfect selves.

We could, of course, all *be* perfect if we could only muster up the energy to complete the list of shoulds. Let's see, how does that go? I should work more, I should work less, I should spend more time with the kids, I should be making a financial contribution to the family, I should be able to get more done since I'm home all day, I should be better organized, I should keep a neater house, I should spend more time with my parents, I should be doing community volunteer work, I really should do better with my family's diet, I should be thinner, and on and on and on.

Oh, and the *should list* doesn't just include things we should be doing right now, a lot of us expand it to include all the things we should have done in the past. I found out I'm not the only one that likes to go back and beat herself up about how I should have done something differently. Woulda, coulda, shoulda, you know the mantra.

The *should list* is a mile long and we're convinced that true happiness will descend upon us when it's all checked off.

FLASH

The perfect thing isn't the key to happiness;
it's in the way of happiness.

You know what? I've talked with real women about when they were the happiest and not a single one ever even mentioned anything that involved being perfect. Nowhere did I hear, "I was happier when my house was cleaner, when I worked harder, was more organized," or any other version of doing it nicer, prettier, or better. So it appears, that in addition to annoying the rest of us, perfection isn't very memorable in terms of life experiences and doesn't make the perfectee any happier either. That's because the perfect thing is all about trying to achieve some image we think we *should be* striving for. It has nothing to do with actually enjoying things.

So, where did their happiness come from? It wasn't feeding the hungry or winning the lottery. It was just a few simple things:

Women are the happiest when they know they matter, when

they know that what they're doing with their time counts for something. It doesn't have to be changing the world. It doesn't even have to be fun, easy, or highly paid; it just has to make a difference to *someone*.

The other times women cite as the happiest are when they're a part of something, when they're connected to other people. Their fondest memories are about being part of a group that was just as interested and excited about whatever it was as they were.

And lastly, when women talk about the best times of their lives, it wasn't when they were doing everything. It was when they could put all that pressure aside and just enjoy doing one thing for a moment.

We've put ourselves last on our own priority lists. And we deserve better than that.

CHAPTER TWO

The Perfect Thing

"I can't go to bed at night until I've finished everything. There's no point even trying because I won't be able to fall asleep until it's all done."

—Myra, age fifty-four, self-employed and mother of two college-age daughters

THE QUEEN OF PERFECT

When I think of someone that's just the perfect mother, career gal, hostess, housekeeper, or whatever, my first reaction is:

A. Can you imagine how stressed-out she must be trying to maintain this facade?

B. Poor thing, it's a shame she can't enjoy the finer things in life.

C. I'm glad my family doesn't have to live with someone that anal retentive.

D. Compare myself to her and then get depressed because I don't measure up.

I had an experience a few years back that first got me questioning this whole perfect thing. It was one of the first times I ever worked with JoAnn.

I had sold my first training program to her company and we spent the week on the West Coast observing the sessions. Up until this point I had been fairly intimidated by JoAnn. Here she was, this big-time VP, all of her underlings always talked about how smart she was, and during the week I found out that she was married and had a son in high school who was getting straight As. Needless to say, she looked to me like one of those women who has it all together and makes the rest of us feel like crap. Throughout the week I had witnessed a parade of great jewelry and, as best I could tell, to top it all off she was nice. Ugh!

I was a young sales rep—back when I thought youth was a bad thing—working for a small start-up company and trying to convince JoAnn that she should go with us rather than the well-established firm she had been using. I had only recently graduated to an all-leather briefcase, so I felt completely out of my league.

I did have a backup plan though; I was going to introduce her to our trainer, Charlotte*. She was closer to JoAnn's age, had a lot more experience than I did, and frankly I thought she was perfect. She never spoke a wrong word, never had a hair out of place, was late, or unprepared. She worked as a highly

*Name changed to protect the semi-innocent

paid sales trainer six or eight days a month, so that she could devote the rest of her time to being room mother, den mother, and for all I knew making costumes for the entire school play. She once told me how she always made sure she had several casseroles in the fridge for her family to heat up at a moment's notice in case she was ever late. That way the family would always have a balanced meal on time. If casseroles don't represent a perfect person I don't know what does. Charlotte was a perfect mother even when she wasn't home. I thought she and JoAnn were made for each other.

I'll spare you the boring business part of the week—it went fine. Charlotte did her part and everyone loved her as usual. She paraded *her* nice jewelry, enthralled the trainees with her brilliance, and was her perfect self.

We were all staying at the same hotel so we went out to dinner together at night. Sure enough, JoAnn and Charlotte did have a lot in common and they made pleasant conversation with each other. I remember thinking, *One day, I'll be like them.*

At the end of the week JoAnn and I discovered we were on the same flight and JoAnn got our tickets switched so that we could sit next to each other. There was nowhere to hide now; surely she was going to find out that I wasn't all I had pretended to be. Sure I could get it together and act sophisticated for a fifteen-minute period and make a comment or two at dinner, but this was a four-hour flight, with no movie!

At a loss for what to talk about, I brought up Charlotte, whom I was sure she hit it off with; after all, perfect people love to be around each other, don't they? JoAnn said, "Oh she was fine, she did a good job this week, but I'm glad she's not flying back with us." Here it comes I thought . . . she wanted to get me alone so she could tell me all the reasons why she wouldn't do business with us. Putting on my best sales rep smile, as I watched my commission dollars being sucked out the plane window, I said, "Oh and why is that?" "Well," she answered, "if she had been on this flight I never would have switched seats to be next to her, I would have just let her walk on back to her seat. She's too perfect for me. Who wants to spend four hours with that?"

You could have picked up my jaw off the tray table. I looked at her stunned, and I think that for a moment she thought I was having some sort of seizure.

FLASH

Trying to be perfect will not make people like you more; it makes them like you less.

I had thought that the closer I got to perfect the better my life would be. **WRONG!** Not only is being perfect too much work and impossible to achieve, it makes you flat-out lonely, because the closer you get, the less other people like you. It doesn't matter what you're trying to perfect—your work, your mothering, your home, your body, your cooking, or heaven forbid, all of the above. The principle is the same: Nobody wants to be around perfection—or you.

Sure they may envy you, but they will also talk about you behind your back to their normal friends every time they see a crack in your armor. Now that I think back to Charlotte, I realize that I didn't actually like her at all. In fact, just being around her made me think less of myself. Was that the kind of feeling I wanted to evoke from people—annoyance and feeling lousy about themselves?

What would I say if Charlotte died? I would feel bad, of course, but you can be sure I wouldn't fly out and make a touching eulogy. I would probably send her family a nice note about what a hardworking professional she was and that would be it! Pretty pathetic, when you realize that she probably worked night and day at being this perfect person in the hope that others around her would appreciate her efforts. All I could muster up was annoyance.

You may think I've made a huge leap here based on just one incident, but I don't think so. Consider these scenarios:

1. You lock yourself out of the car one day at the gas station; you have on no makeup and ratty sweats. Who would you rather see drive up?

    -   Your ex-neighbor, the one that walked around with baby urp all over her shirt the entire time you knew her.

    Or

- Your husband's ex-girlfriend on her way to the country club.

2. Everyone in your office has to go to a meeting two hours away. Who would you rather ride with?

   - The recipient of last year's perfect attendance award.

     Or

   - The woman who got caught doing an imitation of the boss at the company Christmas party.

3. One of your children is throwing a screaming fit in the checkout aisle. Who would you rather have behind you in line?

   - The woman whose child just skipped a grade.

     Or

   - The mother of the "biter" from preschool.

4. You're on vacation and realize you left your electric blanket on, wadded up at the foot of your bed. Which neighbor would you rather ask to go into your bedroom and turn it off?

   - The one whose home was on last year's holiday tour.

     Or

   - The one who uses her formal dining room to sort the laundry.

5. Your husband just informed you that you'd better get a friend to go to that antiques show with you because he has a big ball game to watch. Whose number do you dial?

- Your old college roommate who manages a couple's communication retreat business with her husband.

Or

- Your coworker who told you her husband's mistress was a remote control named Sony.

You get the point. I told you this book was about doing less, not more, so the first thing I'm going to ask you to do is actually to quit doing something. . . .

Quit being your fake self!

You know what I mean, that person you think you should be. The pressure we put on ourselves to maintain our perfect image really is amazing. One woman I interviewed actually told me,

"I feel like I've divided myself up into little compartments and can only open them up one at a time based on who I'm with."

Talk about not being true to yourself! How can this poor woman possibly be herself when she's spending all her time trying to live up to everyone else's expectations? All I can say is I don't know how she did it. There is no way I would be smart enough to remember what role I'm supposed to play and when. Much less have the energy to pull it off. Besides that, how dysfunctional is it to turn into a different woman for every situation you find yourself in?

I'm not saying we should all start going to the mall in our underwear, but this whole image thing has gone too far. It's exhausting and frankly the rest of us don't find it too endearing either. Be your real self. Admit something is wrong with you. I don't know what it is, but there's something. Admitting it will go further than you can believe.

That's what my friend Jennie found out. Before I tell you what happened to her, I have to tell you what she was like beforehand. Perfect doesn't even begin to describe Jennie. When I met her she was thirty years old, knockout gorgeous, had a great job, and was married to a banking executive. I met her because she worked for one of my biggest customers. She was a sales manager, always at the top of the numbers, all her people thought (knew) she was just perfect, and as best I could tell she had never in her whole life been unprepared for anything.

Even more depressing, Jennie looks so great that strangers actually come up to her in the airport and ask where she gets her hair cut. As far as her wardrobe goes, I have never seen anyone more coordinated. She's perfect for every occasion, never overdressed, never underdressed. She's the kind of woman that can pull off that big scarf thing. Somehow, despite these annoying characteristics I grew to like her and we became friends.

Then the unthinkable happened, Jennie got sick. Jennie didn't just get sick, Jennie got cancer. And to make it worse, unbeknownst to the rest of us, her personal life had taken a dramatic turn just a few weeks earlier. It seemed that Jennie's perfect marriage wasn't as perfect as we all thought. After much deliberation, Jennie had reached the conclusion that she had made the wrong choice ten years ago and was ready to undo it. She had asked her husband for a divorce.

Divorce and cancer. Both pieces of news hit the company gossip circuit at the same time. As Jennie described it to me, "Lisa, I couldn't believe it. I was afraid everyone would be whispering about me behind my back. But instead there was a line of people outside my office door, waiting to talk to me. I couldn't believe how much people opened up to me after they found out I had problems too. It just showed me that everyone has one thing, and once they know you have one too, they start becoming your real friend."

I am happy to say that Jennie's cancer is in remission and she has maintained those real friends she found when she was sick. She's still gorgeous and does a great job, but now she's real. Once everyone knew she was human, they went from just working with her to really knowing her. I hope that your one thing isn't nearly as bad as hers, but whatever it is, be up front about it. Even revealing the littlest things about your life that aren't perfect will make you more approachable.

I was reading an article about Katie Couric's ex-nanny the other day. Since she was no longer in Katie's employ, she felt it was appropriate to blab to all the tabs about Katie's secret life. The sum total of her titillating gossip was that on the weekends Katie sometimes goes all day without taking a shower and drinks milk out of the container while standing in front of the fridge.

I've always liked Katie, but now I loved her. She is one of us. Poor Katie has to be up at God knows what hour to be on camera in full makeup first thing in the morning and we all know she has two children. She had already revealed on the air that she knows firsthand the torture of trying to get rid of a two-year-old's pacifier. And the worst thing her ex-nanny can say is that she wants to sit around in sweats all day on the weekend! I don't know if anyone ever didn't like her, but after reading that I felt like she was my soul mate.

Katie's real self is why everyone felt so genuinely bad for her when she lost her husband. Which brings to mind a certain other morning celebrity who subjected us to her and her family's perfectdom once too often (cherublike children *and* a Christmas album were too much for most of us). Well, when she went through a marital crisis of a different nature a few years back, she didn't evoke quite the same response. Rather than sympathy, snickers were more like it. In fact, as I seem to recall, that crack in the armor got more tabloid coverage than space aliens. Point made.

So whether you drink your milk out of the carton or your

husband just lost his job, admit it and join the rest of us. I'm
not talking about whining here; that will drive friends away in
droves. I'm talking about good-naturedly being yourself. I think
you'll find this takes much less energy than living up to any
image you've been trying to craft for yourself.

WHO TURNED THAT THING ON ANYWAY?

When I was a little girl dreaming about my future, I:

A. Looked to the lives of real people as role models.

B. Thoroughly investigated all the options open to me, weighing the pros and cons of each one.

C. Knew that unforeseen events and setbacks would play a big part in it.

D. Conjured up little fantasies with my friends that were in no way based in reality.

Some of you may be more adaptable than I am, but I have a hard time accepting it when everything doesn't go as planned. I just can't stand it when I have something perfect all planned out and then reality jumps in and ruins it.

My career certainly fell into that category. It was turning out to be a lot more drudgery and a lot less excitement than I had expected. Drudgery had been my mother's and other women's lives, it wasn't supposed to be mine. My life was going to be different. I wasn't going to just have a job, I was going to have a career. Careers were supposed to be fun, weren't they?

⚡

FLASH

That's why it's called work and they pay you.
If it was nonstop fun and thrills, you would
pay them and call it Disneyland.

Why was I so surprised? Where did I get this idea that work would be so great? What woman did I actually know who had the kind of career I dreamed about? Another flash . . . I didn't know one single woman growing up who had the kind of life I dreamed about. So where did I get this picture?

Was it the Women's Movement, my mother, college, or a well-meaning guidance counselor? I'm sure they all played a part in molding my great ambitions, but where did the vivid picture come from? I should be embarrassed to admit this, but I think that the picture actually came from television.

I grew up in the '70s and television was reality to me. To this day, I still believe if it says "*based* on a true story" that the woman who lost her baby in a snowstorm looked exactly like Valerie Bertanelli when it was happening.

I remember watching the *Mary Tyler Moore* show when I was a kid. Mary really had the life, didn't she? She worked in television, was always going on some exciting date, and she had that great apartment. Mary was everything my mother and the other women I knew were not. Mary was fun! I was going to be Mary Richards.

Thinking back on it, I realize that good ole Mary had a metal desk in the middle of the newsroom, she had to call her boss Mr. Grant, and she had to go into his office whenever he buzzed for her. As for that great apartment, she rented it and had to sleep on a sofa bed. I think the best things Mary had going for her were lots of dates and a great wardrobe. Is it any wonder she appealed to me at age twelve?

Combine my good friend Mary with a few *Dynasty* episodes, *Dallas, One Day at a Time*, and some assorted soap operas and I had the basis for a career path. I based my life on television and was then shocked to find out it didn't work that way in real life. Go figure!

I talked to JoAnn about my career woes and her first response was, "Of course it's hard, it's work. What did you expect, fun?"

Why had she learned the lesson and I hadn't? Her background gave me some clues. JoAnn may have been the good little girl when she was growing up in the wonderful '50s, but she let me in on a few little secrets about that grand and glorious time in Americana.

Contrary to popular belief, a lot of women worked, even back then and JoAnn's mother was one of them. Her parents ran a restaurant on the edge of town. To hear her describe it, it was one of those sit-down, fried food, waitress-with-the-notepad kind of places that got a big crowd when the mill changed shifts. It was open for lunch and dinner, which meant her parents worked pretty much around the clock, from early in the morning until late at night.

Work wasn't fun for her parents. It was just plain hard. When work turned out to be hard for JoAnn she wasn't surprised. She'd seen that picture close up her whole life. She didn't have a little box showing her a different one.

FLASH

The perfect picture in your head never includes the hard parts.

I didn't know any real women with the kind of career I dreamed of. All I knew were mothers.

Come to think of it, the most pleasant surprise of my life has been how fun and exciting being a mother is for me. I expected motherhood to be hard work, boring, and no fun. Why? As the oldest of four, I had seen it all firsthand: the late nights, the crying, the bills, the earaches, the driving, and the mess. Remember the orange shag? That was what I expected, and as any mother knows, that's what I got. But it wasn't a surprise.

The surprise was when the baby did sleep through the night, when there was enough money to pay the bills, when my husband did pitch in—and the biggest surprise of all was the fun. I had never in my wildest dreams expected it to be fun. I thought it might ultimately be fulfilling and rewarding, but fun? Never. It was something I was supposed to do.

Who found motherhood more work and less fun than she imagined? JoAnn. Her parents were older when she was born and so busy running the restaurant they didn't have a lot of time for her. They had two older sons and JoAnn suspects she may have been a midlife surprise. The result was that although she had a mother, she spent very little time observing mothering firsthand. But wait, there were a few families she spent some time with. Who were they? The Cleavers, the Nelsons, and the Andersons. Even today, JoAnn says that whenever she vacuums she can't shake the feeling she should don pumps and pearls to do it right.

I'm not going to make a big case against television here. My kids go over that thirty-minute limit all the time so I can't take the high ground on this one. It's more than just television. It's the unrealistic pictures we get into our head of the way things *should* be. It's when we never saw it up close, every day, for real.

Or maybe we did see, we just didn't think it applied to us. My friend Tracy says,

"When I was growing up my mom had to handle everything because my dad was always at work. He never even went on vacation with us. My mom was always tired and frustrated, so I was sure I didn't want her life. So instead I ended up spending all my time at work, just like my dad. It never dawned on me for one minute that by giving up her life I was getting his. Somehow, when *he came dragging home too tired to speak every night, I never made the connection that one day that would be me."*

She saw it, but she just ignored it. Guess I'm not the only one who hatched her plan in La-La Land. And it's not like everyone's out there flaunting all the messy details and behind-the-scenes stuff. Lots of people's lives look perfect when we only see a little piece of it. Hell, mine looks great.

If I didn't tell you any different, you might never know that my phone has been cut off twice because I have lost the bills. You know how I lost them? Both times it was in December when I was having a big holiday party. In order to present the perfect front that was so important to me in those days, I scooped up all the assorted papers we keep permanently on our kitchen counter and put them away, somewhere. Somewhere really safe that has not revealed itself to this day. The phone company, being one of the more aggressive bill collectors, took action first.

There I stood in my perfect house looking like a model of organizational skills, when the reality was I had not only lost several of our bills, but I was so disorganized I didn't notice it until I couldn't get a dial tone.

Next time you look at someone else's little picture, remember, that's just the part they let you see. I don't care if it's work, motherhood, or a stupid cocktail party; the whole picture always includes a hard part.

As for JoAnn, she was and continues to be a really good

mother. I know her son, and even if she wasn't making sure I got this in, I would tell you myself, he's great. Not perfect you notice, but great. It's not so much what JoAnn did or didn't do, or even how she did it. It's how she felt about it. JoAnn tells me that she has very few regrets about her mothering; I should be so lucky. But she does have one biggie:

> *"If I had to do it all over again, the one thing I would do differently is to enjoy it more. I was trying so hard to make it perfect, I couldn't enjoy it."*

I told you I don't want to make more work for you and I don't. I just want you to enjoy it more. So **lose the picture**. I don't know where you got it or what it's of, but I bet it wasn't anything you saw on a firsthand basis. If you think it was, check again. Are you sure you saw it all or are you just remembering the parts you liked?

Once JoAnn talked with other mothers and realized that June and Ward were actors who got paid on Friday just like the rest of us, she started to ease up on herself. For me, after I admitted to myself once and for all that work was work and I wasn't about to take over Ewing Oil, I could relax and enjoy the good parts with a sense of humor.

One of the ways we were both able to lose the perfect picture was to talk with real women about their real lives. That's another reason why I would like you to open up and quit being your fake self. It gives the rest of us permission to do the same.

You see, when we're all presenting our fake self, we're just on the outside looking in. We're not showing—or seeing—the big picture.

If you've been comparing your life to unrepresentative samples you saw of someone else's, or TV shows that took a week of shooting to get twenty-three minutes, or some fantasy you conjured up for yourself when your parents' lives didn't look too good—QUIT.

Stop beating yourself up every time your world doesn't match the picture you've got in your head. Those pictures never include the tough parts so using them as your benchmark is skewing your whole perception. Accept the fact that reality is going to insist on rearing her ugly head on a regular basis. Recognize her for what she is—real life. Not personal failure on your part.

Nobody ever enjoyed anything when they had a picture in their head of something better.

"YOU REALLY SHOULD..."

When I get advice from everyone else on what I *should* be doing I:

A. Turn a deaf ear because I know that society is putting way too much pressure on women.

B. Realize that they are only trying to demonstrate their knowledge by offering me advice.

C. Am grateful that they are keeping up with things so that I don't have to waste my time thinking about such mundane matters.

D. Know that I must really be a mess if other people are able to spot so many of my personal inadequacies.

I may have convinced you to let up for a moment, but don't count on the rest of the world to give you a break. Everywhere we turn there's someone giving us advice on how to be better. Whether it's Home and Garden TV, the latest parenting book, or a Slim Fast ad, everywhere we look is another example of where we're falling short.

We're bombarded with a dizzying array of helpful suggestions on how to improve ourselves. Do this. Do that. The more you can cram into a day the better. Don't be a slackard, get a good day planner and you can do it all. The world's your oyster, it's whatever you want . . . wife, mother, or juggler in a three-ring circus.

We've heard everything from developing a family mission statement to preparing a month's worth of casseroles in advance to putting a little basket near where we sort our mail. I for one know that if I hear one more expert tell me that waking up an hour earlier is an effective time-management strategy, I will scream. Going through life as a zombie and prematurely aging myself through sleep deprivation is not my idea of better.

It's supposed to be a life, not a road race.

Most of the women I know are doing pretty doggone well for themselves. Yet, the rest of the world feels compelled to point out every possible aspect of our inadequacies and then proceed to tell us what to do about it. If you've been able to avoid this trend, all I can say is, either you are more evolved than the rest of us or you have been living under a rock.

My friend Donna says,

"It's almost like I've got that old army refrain in my head. You know, 'Be all you can be.' I've heard the best way to do everything and so every time I cut myself a little slack on something I feel lazy. If there's more to do, I should be doing it."

She's got the army refrain driving her, but remember that ad with the woman who could, "Bring home the bacon, fry it up in a pan, and never let him forget he's a man" all within the same twenty-four-hour period? Well, I don't do it all in twenty-four hours, I just spend my days having other people tell me I should. Consider this litany of advice I was actually offered during the brief span of one day:

7:30 A.M.

"If you will just take the time to get out and caulk these windows every year, you won't have this problem again. You really should make your home a priority. It's your biggest investment, you owe it to yourself to take care of it."

—Shouted down from a ladder by the man fixing my rotting woodwork

10:30 A.M.

"Think of yourself and make the time to exercise every day, you'd feel so much better. Your health should be one of your top priorities. If you don't have that you don't have anything."

—From a note from the instructor at the gym wondering where I've been

12:15 P.M.

"If you will just set aside a half an hour every night to monitor her homework, it will make a big difference. Your child's academics really is the most important thing."

—During a phone call with my daughter's teacher

3:15 P.M.

"You're really going to have to do a more thorough job with your follow-up. This is a big client and I wouldn't think I should have to remind you how important this is. The people that pay our salaries should be the priority here."

—The verdict on a project I thought I'd finished

5:15 P.M.

"Your husband is your partner for life. Make your marriage a priority or you won't have it. Set aside time and let him know how important he is."

> —From a magazine article in the pediatrician's waiting room

8:10 P.M.

"Lisa, you have to be more organized about your finances. It's all about paying yourself first. You should spend some more time on this, you'd really see the payoff later."

> —A phone call from my stockbroker brother reminding me that I haven't saved enough money this year

Well, if all these people are so gosh darn concerned about me, they can come over to my house, cook my family dinner, read to my kids, and wrap my mother-in-law's birthday present while they pour champagne into my bubble bath. Oh, and on that gift, make sure you sign the card so it looks like my husband picked it out for her himself.

The worst thing about all this advice is that, because he was the last one to chime in, I totally lost it with my brother and hung up on the one person who probably does have my best interest at heart.

FLASH

Perfect is a collection of "should" lists we get from everyone else.

You know why somebody keeps telling you whatever it is *should* be so important? It's because it's the most important thing in the world to them. Whether it's the way they earn their living, spend their time, or prove their worth to humanity, just because it's tops on their priority list they assume it should hold the same place of honor on yours.

All I can say is—there's only so much room at the top. If you look back at my little array of suggestions, there's not a bit of it that's bad advice. Maybe it's not the quality, but the quantity that's so overwhelming. How do we deal with the onslaught?

First and foremost, accept the fact that there's simply not time in the world to rotate your tires, grow fresh herbs, change the air-conditioning filters, work all the major muscle groups, plan your financial future, and liberally apply sunscreen every time you leave the house. At least not if you're going to insist on sleeping, working, raising a family, or other such trivial matters along the way.

Once you realize that, I suggest considering the source when deciding how to respond. Let's look at who's offering us all this help:

First there's the *Hired Help*, the advice from the experts. I use that term loosely to mean anyone personally hired by you such as plumbers, baby-sitters, accountants, doctors, house-keepers, shrinks, and painters, or anyone in the employ of an establishment you do business with.

You wouldn't think this type of advice would be annoying, but all it takes to humble me is for my auto mechanic to ask when the last time I changed the oil was. I can only hang my head in shame mumbling something about how I have to travel a lot.

It helps to remember that, technically, these people work for *you*. I don't care if it's your doctor, broker, or the clerk at your local garden center. It's their job to give you advice. And you don't always have to pay attention, because it's also their job to offer it over and over again.

That's not to say it's all worth listening to. Just because they have their name on their shirt doesn't necessarily mean they know what they're talking about. They may have their own agenda operating. Another thing to keep in mind is that these professionals don't always follow their own advice. Case in point: I once worked with a group of psychiatric hospitals that employed the biggest bunch of nutcases I've ever met in my life.

Most of the pros are just trying to make a living or impress everyone with how smart they are. So ignore the idiots and let the rest of them do their jobs. I'm sure you're even better at yours.

Then there's the advice of a more overt and personal nature, from the *Should Committee*. This includes everyone from complete strangers to members of your own family who can't keep from commenting on how you're managing your life. They're the quit slouching, eat your vegetables, and put a hat on that baby crew. They may insist they're offering it for your own good, but I've noticed some suspicious themes.

For one thing, their advice is inevitably about something they're either done with, have yet to do, or mistakenly think they're doing well. I've found this to be especially true when it pertains to how you *should* handle infants, toddlers, or teenagers. The strongest opinions are usually voiced by those that don't have to live with one.

The other thing I've noticed about this advice is that it is largely unsolicited. You have to wonder—is their own life so boring that judging yours is the only excitement they get? Or perhaps they're so helplessly lonely that this is the only way they can connect with people. Or maybe everybody else they know is sick of it and so they moved on to you. Whatever the reason, I suspect it has more to do with their need to give the advice rather than your need to receive it.

If you didn't ask and the helper doesn't have a proven track record for sage and timely advice, consider it white noise. You may have a few people who tactfully give much-needed advice when asked, but a lot of the stuff coming your way can be safely ignored. Because rejecting it outright only tends to heighten their efforts, the method I like best is to nod gravely, pause for a moment and then respond with, "Thanks, you've really given me something to think about." This effectively ends the conversation and still falls within the guidelines of the polite behavior most of us try to adhere to during family reunions.

There's also the *Always Available Advice*, the advice that's not directly aimed at you but is just out there in the form of books, magazines, and TV shows. It seems a bit ludicrous to let the how-to industry get to us, but I can't tell you how many women I've met who feel guilty because they haven't been able to follow a certain blonde's advice on the perfect holiday. Let me remind you that this stuff is entertainment masquerading as advice. They've done the work, so enjoy it. You don't have to duplicate it. And remember, most of those home improvement couples on TV aren't really married.

Whether advice is coming from the handyman, your mother-in-law, or some efficiency expert, don't take it personally because the rest of us are getting it too. Try a few of these screening techniques to help you wade through it all:

1. Ask the advice giver what bad thing will happen to you or the people you care about if you don't do whatever it is. If the worst-case scenario is you have to hire them back to clean up your mess or remind you again, then rest easy knowing that you secured their gainful employment for another day.

2. Praise the advisor for being so conscientious on this topic. Because you could never keep up with such trivial matters

yourself, ask them if they could please call you the next time they caulk, paint, or rotate to remind you to do the same.

3. Explain to the advisor that you are just too busy right now and that they will have to repeat this advice on at least three separate occasions before you can consider listening to it.

4. Ask the advisor point-blank what's in it for them if you follow their advice. Dismiss anyone who can't look you in the eye when they answer.

5. Invite the advisor to peruse your to-do list and circle any items they would like to handle for you so you can free up the time to follow their advice.

6. Tell the advisor that you're trying to achieve happiness not perfection, so all suggestions must be in the form of a written proposal detailing exactly how much happier you will be by implementing them.

7. If you're still considering the advice after all of the above, it's probably good, so take it. But not before you congratulate yourself for being a very smart cookie indeed. You have surrounded yourself with competent people and have wisely delegated the worrisome details to them. Bravo to you.

The irony of my giving you this *advice* is not lost on me. So if anything I say fails to meet the above criteria, feel free to disregard it.

THE CASE AGAINST HOUSEWORK, DIETING, AND OTHER SHOULDS

When I look at the list of things I *should* do on any given day I:

A. Know that I can pick and choose based on what's really important to me.

B. Realize that all the people I need to do something for really care about me, not just the things I do for them.

C. Look forward to doing each and every menial task on the list because I know I'm making life better for myself and others.

D. Feel completely overwhelmed and hope that it doesn't take me until midnight to get it all done.

I think I've made a pretty good case against trying to be perfect already, it doesn't make us any happier, no one enjoys trying to live up to it, no one wants to be around it, no one actually does it, and everybody else made it up. That's enough for me to abandon it, but some of you may have a stronger work ethic and aren't going to cut yourself any slack.

I won't presume to tell you how to live your life, (at least not this early in the book). I am going to take this opportunity to get up on my high horse and lecture you about a few things I think have absolutely no bearing on your lifetime happiness and *should* therefore be struck from your list.

The first one to go has got to be housework. My friend Teressa's got a great perspective on this. She went back to teaching this year after ten years of being at home. During her sabbatical she gave birth to and raised three daughters, taught them how to walk erect, use the potty, feed themselves, and eventually march off to school alone. Having accomplished this, she was now ready to return to work. I think a vacation would have been more in order, but back to a paying job she went. As she says,

"The summer before I went back, I really tried to get everything organized because I knew it was going to be a tough year. That last week, the girls went to my in-law's and I went into overdrive. I cleaned, vacuumed, and did every piece of laundry in the entire house. For the first time in our lives there wasn't one thing that needed doing. The day before they came back, I was packing away the last of the clothes when I realized it was all done. I sat down, looked around and thought—So what? Nobody was any happier, nobody was any smarter, and nothing in our lives had changed at all.

It's been a really hectic year all right, but whenever things seem totally out of control I always try to remember that moment and it helps. I don't want my girls to think that cleaning is a priority. Housework doesn't make them any happier . . . I do."

· ⚡ ·

FLASH

Your example is creating the next generation's "should" list.

· ·

Among the many things I can thank my own mother for, a big one is abysmally low housekeeping standards. No matter how bad my house gets, it could never look worse than hers.

Our house was always a pit. My mother taught school full-time and ran a household that included four kids, a dog, assorted cats, and a husband whose mother had never trained him to do his own wash. Somewhere along the line, she realized she could drive herself crazy doing it all or she could just give up. Cleaning services were not in the budget, so she made the obvious choice and surrendered. In hindsight, I suspect that it was probably a guilt-ridden compromise given the standards of the time and a difficult one for someone who was by nature a very neat person. I went through her personal things after she died and was shocked at how clean and orderly they were. But the rest of us must have been too much for one woman to handle, so she lived with the mess. Fingerprints were on the wall, dog food was on the floor, Kool-Aid was on the ugly furniture, and the laundry was never done.

You know what? Not one single bad thing happened to our

family because of it. After she died, we ripped out the crummy carpet, donated the furniture, hired an industrial cleaning service, and sold the damn house. If she had lived, she could have done the same thing herself.

I can't tell you how many women I've met who, although they are wonderful people, friends, mothers, wives, and other things that actually matter, continue to beat themselves up because you can't see your underwear in the shine off their kitchen floors. These women are made absolutely miserable because their mothers, or worse, their mothers-in-law, kept better houses than they do. Do the next generation a favor and lower your standards. Besides . . . **Housework is never done because the act of actually living in your house undoes your efforts.** This frustrating process puts you at constant odds with your family, because they continue to mess up your work.

If you can't live with it or afford to pay someone else to take care of it, the only solution I can think of is to trade off with a friend. Once a week you can clean each other's houses. This accomplishes several things:

1. You will have that wonderful experience of walking in the door to a clean house.

2. You'll realize that other families are worse slobs than yours.

3. You won't have to worry about cleaning the rest of the week because it will only be a few days until "the help" comes.

4. Your family can then proceed to mess up her work, not yours.

I don't know about you, but I find someone else's mess much less depressing than my own.

While we're on the subject of domesticity, I would like to add something specific about cooking and laundry. As far as I'm concerned, these two are the worst of the lot. Unless your whole family is naked and on IV's, you can never get caught up on either one. Try as you might, they will insist on wearing and dirtying the clothes and eating the food so you'll have to start all over again. I for one think you have to question any job that takes longer to do than it does to undo. In my family we have solved part of the problem by purchasing a month's supply of underwear for everyone. As far as kitchen duty goes, all I can say is, paper plates and a can opener get a lot more use than my Cuisinart does these days.

Beyond housework there are a few other **shoulds** that I think bear mentioning. Even if you can't remove them from your list, here are some suggestions to make them more bearable:

The social graces

My grandmother will turn over in her grave at this one, but I think we should all make a pact not to write thank-you notes. Well, truthfully my friends and I couldn't quite leave our upbringing behind, so we came up with a system that works beautifully. Whenever we give someone a gift we take a little piece of leftover wrapping paper and scribble on it:

Dear Lisa, Thank you for the lovely gift. I appreciate it. Love, _____

The blank is for the recipient to sign her name. We put it right on the front of the gift in place of a greeting card. Before she opens the gift, she signs it and hands the "thank-you note" back. We consider it part of the gift and find it much more endearing than anything Hallmark ever came up with.

Entertaining

I used to be guilty of going a little overboard on this one myself. But now that I've had children, if you ever get an invite from me, it includes asking you to pick up the food on the way.

JoAnn, however, is another story. When we first discussed this topic she was still clinging to the belief that a guest didn't feel fully welcome unless she prepared a theme meal complete with decorated place cards.

JoAnn would have continued down this worrisome path were it not for an invitation she received recently. She and her husband were asked to a dinner party by one of her clients. She had never met his wife before, so she had no idea what to expect. Well, wouldn't you know it, JoAnn was invited to dinner by the only woman alive that could outdo her. Talk about a hostess with the mostest, everything was perfect, from the crystal and flowers, to the rack of lamb and the individual soufflés. To hear JoAnn tell it, it looked like a magazine layout. Her response to all of this work done on her behalf?

"I spent the whole evening wondering how she possibly did it all. I could never do anything that elegant. I don't have the house, the serving pieces, or even the kitchen to turn out something like that. I went home feeling like I didn't measure up. I hope people don't feel like that when they come to my house."

Think about it, what do you want people to say in the car on the way home, "Can you believe all the work she did, that spread looked too good to eat," or, "Wow, I've never laughed so hard in my life, what a great time"? Your friends want to see you, not your backside poking out from the oven.

Dieting

You can't talk about women and the perfect thing without at least mentioning our bodies. I myself have spent the better part of the last decade either pregnant, fat, or both, so I've had considerable experience with this issue. While I can't honestly say that I'm completely at peace with it, I did have an experience last summer that took a little bit of the pressure off.

I was at the pool with my kids one day wearing my usual black, skirted, tummy-control-panel swimsuit. I still had twenty pounds left from a child that was practically ready to go off the diving board and so my waistline and upper things were not fit for public consumption. As I hovered underwater with my tot strategically held in front of me, I took a good look at a few of my more fit neighbors. You know, those women that still find time to work out and probably get their legs waxed on a regular basis. Once I got past ogling their thinness I realized they didn't look *that* great. They had the same jiggly arms, loose tummies, and dimpling thighs I did, only smaller.

What a shock! I had thought that the only thing keeping me from looking like the nineteen-year-old lifeguard was my own slothlike behavior. But this crew was evidence that age and gravity are two variables none of us can control. After all, they had dieted and exercised themselves to death, and they still looked like a group of fortysomething women who'd had a few kids. Thin ones for sure, but the lifeguard remained alone in her perfectness. Quit ruining the best times of your life by worrying about how you look. No one really cares.

So, there you have it, my personal contribution to reducing your *should list*. We're all putting on our baggy sweats, coming over to your messy house, ordering double cheese pizza, and having a great time, secure in the knowledge that we don't even have to send you a thank-you. Sounds like more fun than some floral filled wine tasting to me.

"JUST FINE" ISN'T EXACTLY WHAT I WAS GOING FOR HERE

A lot of you may be reeling at this point and think I'm suggesting we resign ourselves to mediocrity in every endeavor of life. After all, once you've heard "anything worth doing is worth doing well," it's hard to let up. My friend Barbara wasn't about to settle for less. She's an interior decorator and perfect is what she goes for each and every day.

> *"I'd never make a living if I told people it was just going to look OK when I was done. And besides that, I want it to look perfect. In fact, I don't feel like I've done my job until they use those exact words. When they walk in, look around and say, 'Barbara I love it, it's just perfect,' I feel so proud of myself. No way am I going to give that up."*

I for one wouldn't dream of asking her to. It's how she earns a living and she's great at it. She will traipse over hill and dale in search of the perfect plaid and doesn't consider a visit to a fabric store complete until she has personally inspected every bolt in the place, even if it includes going out back to see what just came in on the truck. Her clients are always thrilled with the results and more importantly; Barbara likes it while she's doing it.

That's one of the differences. When you love it, or at least like it, while you're in the process of doing whatever it is, it's not about trying to achieve some perfect image. It's about doing something you're good at and enjoy. I'm not saying you have to be thrilled with every minute; I'm sure even Barbara gets annoyed when the dye lots don't match, but if you're going through the motions because you think you *should*, I doubt you'll be much happier when you're done.

The other litmus test for the perfect thing is: Does it have a positive effect on you or anyone else? Now be really honest with yourself on this one, because you know how annoying we find those Perfect Queens. So if you're absolutely sure whatever you're obsessing about or working on will have a lasting effect on the events of your life, keep it up. And don't let anybody else tell you any different. Shannon didn't.

When her oldest son was two and a half, Shannon noticed that he wasn't talking as well as the other kids in preschool. She read up on the subject a little and while the books she consulted put him in the normal range, she was still worried. She shared her concerns with her husband, her parents, her doctor, and some friends and they all told her the same thing, "Don't worry, he's just fine."

"Just fine" isn't exactly the benchmark I have set for myself regarding something as important as my kids. And it wasn't what Shannon had in mind either. To make a long story short, she got him to a specialist who determined while there were no major problems, he was a little behind. She taught Shannon how to work with him and he caught up fairly quickly. Shannon wasn't insisting that her son be perfect; she was just making sure she did her best for him. She's not neurotic, there was a little something wrong and it could have been something worse. She might have missed it if she had settled for "just fine."

FLASH

Forget perfect doesn't mean lowering your standards, it means raising them.

Raising them for what really matters and putting your own happiness at the top of the list. You don't deserve less. You deserve more.

You deserve more of those wonderful moments when you're enjoying something so much you say to yourself, "it's perfect." When you can say that, it probably is just perfect. And who doesn't love it when somebody important to us tells us whatever we did was "just perfect?" Those times have nothing to do with the *should list* and striving for some perfect image, those are the times when you actually forgot about that for a minute. The perfect thing I'm referring to isn't the one that makes you feel better, it's the one that makes you feel worse.

I'm not suggesting you abandon perfect because you can't pull it off. I'm sick of people telling us not to be such perfectionists in some condescending way that suggests it's somehow too much for us. It's not too much for us, it's too little. I want you to dump it because you deserve better. You deserve more than just going through the motions of life, you deserve to have a life and forget perfect is where it starts.

The *should list* and *just fine* are about what everybody else thinks. Once you get them out of the way, you can worry about what you think. If you love whatever you're doing or you think it might really matter in the long run, feel free to set your standards a little higher than the *just fine* benchmark. Go for marvelous, fantastic, wonderful, and even fun. In fact, now that we've freed up a little time and brain space by dumping that perfect thing, we can move on to the good stuff.

CHAPTER THREE

Mother Nature Had Something in Mind

"It's not nice to fool Mother Nature."

—*Parkay Margarine advertisement*

THE TRUTH ABOUT DOGS AND CATS

I think my life would be more meaningful if I:

A. Made buckets o' money by being as tough-minded and un-scrupulous as Cruella de Vill.

B. Owned and ran my own small country.

C. Was featured on the cover of *Domestic Goddess* magazine.

D. Knew that what I was doing mattered to someone.

We've all got it into our heads that if we could only make more money, change our jobs, or finally get that dining room set we would be happy. But you know what? When I asked real

women about the best times in their lives, here's what they said
made them really happy:

"Being the top sales manager isn't where I get my thrills. When I feel really satisfied in this job is when I know I'm being a great boss. When I help someone grow professionally or personally, now that's really what matters to me, that's when I know what I do is really important to someone."

—Suzanne, sales manager

"I'm so different now that I'm home with the kids. My life probably seems pretty boring to most people, but to me I feel like it's a chance to do something really important, or at least I think that on the days when it's going well. I can't even remember who that other person was who ran for airplanes and barked orders at people. I'm really my best right now."

—Shannon, a stay-at-home mother with three kids under the age of three

"Some days when I have a million papers to grade and my back is killing me from bending over, I wonder why I keep doing this. But then all of a sudden I'll see one of the kids 'get it' and I'll remember why I became a teacher in the first place."

—Holly, a high school English teacher

"One thing I know for sure is when I look back on this part of my life, I'll know that that little old lady in the nursing home lived a

longer, healthier life because of the way we took care of her. That's really important to me—if I can do that, I've really done something."

—Rachelle, on working in the nursing home business

"The day they put Molly into my arms was the day I knew my life meant something. The world just stopped and suddenly I was somebody's mother. I've had some ups and downs since then, but that day I knew somebody really needed me."

—Susan, on the adoption of her daughter

"It's funny, but one of the things I've come to enjoy most is being a good friend. When somebody's got something great or even something awful to share and I'm the one they call, I know I really matter."

—Debby, who proves it every time I call her

Once again the perfect thing doesn't even register on the radar screen in terms of memorable life experiences.

In spite of these women having some pretty big accomplishments in their lives, the times that meant the most to them were really quite ordinary. It wasn't saving the planet or enjoying the lifestyles of the rich and famous. It wasn't even when they were running the universe from a cell phone beside the pool. It was when they were doing something that mattered to someone.

*It's not what we do, it's the way it connects
to others that's so important to us.*

Besides setting ourselves up for failure with that perfect non-sense, we also got the notion that our accomplishments define our lives. And you know where we got it? That's right! False advertising from the rest of the world.

Just read the obituaries for heaven's sake. The people that accomplish a lot get the big write up. Yet, very rarely do I see some heartfelt quote about how much they meant to someone. Most of us learned this little lesson early on. Remember history class? I learned all about who conquered the new frontier, created the Industrial Age, led the charge against the enemies, or founded a country. You know, the important stuff. Well, maybe I was snoozing in the back of the room, but I don't recall any history teacher of mine ever talking about who actually influenced George Washington to become the man he was. Guess he was so honest about that cherry tree because he was raised by a pack of wolves.

If you don't think we're hung up on this one, then tell me, when we meet someone new why is the first question out of everyone's mouth, "What do you do?" If that isn't defining someone by their accomplishments I don't know what is.

But just doing *things* isn't what makes women tick. We could move a mountain, but we know it doesn't count unless someone needed it moved and says thank-you when we're done.

Accomplishments don't have to require the *approval* of others, that's the stupid *should list* rearing its ugly head. What makes accomplishments meaningful is how we connect with others. In fact, I've heard several women use that exact word "connected" and I don't think they're talking about the ability to get the best tables in fancy restaurants. What they mean is being a part of something—work, community, family—it doesn't matter, the feeling is the same. Women want to know that we make a difference at some point in time to someone. It doesn't have to change the course of humanity, we just want it to count for *something*.

All you teachers, nurses, nannies, and social workers out there can have the last laugh now. Some of us went pretty far out of our way to make sure we didn't end up in those kind of "women jobs." No, we were going to do really important work.

What did I wind up doing? I sold toilet paper for a packaged goods company, or at least until I moved on to the more meaningful business of training salespeople. Guess what my company trained salespeople to do? Call on nurses and demonstrate how their products would assist them in the valuable work of saving people's lives. I also volunteer at my daughter's school helping her teacher shape the future of society by molding young minds. You know what? In my whole boring life, those are two of the high spots.

They're highlights because they matter—and not just to me.

Like a lot of women, I enjoy doing something more if I have a clear picture of who I'm doing it for. In this regard, I must say that my preliminary research on this subject confirms what I've been suspecting for quite some time: We think about our lives differently than men!

Suppose it was your job to vaccinate every child in this world. You know it is going to be a long, difficult job that will require a lifetime of hard work. You are sure to face exhaustion, frustration, anguish, and hardship along the way. What mental picture will you carry with you each and every day that will enable you to get out of bed and face another day of this?

Every single woman I asked answered with a version of the same response—the faces. They always had a mental picture of themselves helping someone and they almost always pictured themselves looking right into their eyes. They pictured holding a sick child, laughing with a smiling and healthy child, comforting a grieving mother, or a mother so grateful her child was alive. They always connected their action to a person.

What did the men picture? My father said a ward full of sick children; my husband said a playground of healthy children; my friend Steve said the acclaim once it was done; my brother said imagining the disease no longer existed. If they pictured the people it was always a large group and they were looking at them from afar, not interacting with them. Not one of them gave that personal, connected answer.

Contrary to what some of my former bosses may have believed, wanting to focus on the personal aspects of our jobs or activities doesn't mean sitting around all day and yakking about what good friends we are. We can accomplish the same things as men, but we just need a different picture to get there.

The men in your life may be a little more relationship-oriented than mine, but I've yet to meet one who looks at things the same way women do. Why is this such a surprise? Just look at the two sexes and you can see we look no more alike than a dog and a cat. If your cat started to bark one day you would be on the phone with David Letterman faster than Whiskers could say *arf*. Yet for some reason, despite our clear physical differences, I always assumed our brains worked the same. Well, truth be told, I always thought ours were just a bit faster, but I am finally just now getting it about how different we are.

And what's more, I think it's all part of Mother Nature's grand plan, so we better not mess with it.

She, or the divine being of your choice, wanted to ensure the survival of the species, so she wired women to be mothers. To be a good mother, or to even try to be any kind of mother at all, you have to spend huge amounts of time shaping and molding another person. You look for every opportunity you can to improve that person, to make a difference in the way they turn out.

You might be thinking, "I'm sure prehistoric women weren't reading Dr. Spock and looking for developmentally appropriate toys. They didn't make themselves crazy trying to make every moment a teaching opportunity." Oh yeah? Well, what do you think would happen to their darling baby if Mummy didn't make sure they knew which berries were yummy and which ones killed you?

Since the dawn of time, mothers have worked tirelessly to produce the best offspring they possibly could. Good ole Mother Nature knew this was a difficult task at best, so she wired us with a burning desire to do it. It's not something we can turn on or off depending on whether or not we have chosen to use it on children.

You don't believe me? Well consider this: Why else would we try to change every man we arc in contact with for any length of time? There is no way that this is a learned behavior, because anyone that has tried to do it more than once knows it is not only an impossible job for the changer (us), but the changee (them) resents the hell out of it.

Why then, do we continue to try and do it? We are preprogrammed with a need to leave a lasting imprint on the face of the world by shaping another person's behavior. And if the man in our life is the only one available? Well, guess what, buddy, you're it!

I spent the early years of my own marriage trying to develop my husband. You can just imagine how thrilled he was with his new wife. Somewhere along the line I gave up. Did I finish the job and move on? Hardly. In fact, I made very little progress at all, I must have just found other places to use my wiring.

He was good enough for me to fall in love with and marry, so he couldn't have needed that much help. I can promise you that he hasn't changed one bit since then. I may come back to my work with him at some later date, but for now he is letting out a big sigh of relief that I have turned my efforts elsewhere.

He didn't need the work, it was *my* need to look at another person and figure out how they could be better, to help them, to alter the course of human events, because that's the way women are wired. It's what makes us count.

What makes it count for men? I think for them it counts if it is difficult, and the harder it is, the more it counts. Connecting it to others is really secondary. It's the work that counts.

Now why are they like this? Well, Mother Nature in her infinite wisdom knew that the really big game, the kind that would feed a tribe for a long, cold winter was harder to track than say, digging up a few bugs from under a rock. So by wiring them with "the harder the better" mentality, she ensured that the lot of them would trek over hill and dale just to outdo one another in the quest for a beast.

I think that this explains why the modern man seems to feel that the more he bellyaches and curses while he's doing something, the more grateful we will be. They think if they moan before, during, and after any favor they do for us, it will count more. Why? Because it proves it was harder and harder is better.

Feel free to show this section of the book to any man in your life, including any whiners that may work for you whether in a spousal or employee role. We women know that if you are going to do it anyway, doing it with a smile on your face makes it count more. Bellyaching makes it count less!

Before you work yourself into a tizzy and think I'm suggesting that the only thing we're good for is raising a pack of cave kids, let's be clear: I'm not. I am saying that women feel their lives are the most meaningful when their actions are connected to others and make a difference in others' lives.

A more cynical woman might take this opportunity to point out that influencing others is a skill that has stood the test of time, whereas the ability to track large game has seen a real decline in marketability lately.

We can't go back to the cave, even if we want to. Maybe we don't really need to change our lives, we can just change the way we feel about them. We need a different picture.

The next time you've got some boring menial task to do— and I mean really *have* to, not *should* do—you know one of those nuisances like making a living or driving the carpool, instead of just focusing on *what* you're doing, I want you to think about *why*. Or better yet, *who*. Who out there, even if it's a stranger, is going to benefit from it?

You might have to stretch a bit, but I have to believe that somebody, somewhere is affected by whatever it is you're slaving away on. We'll talk about how to get them to say thank-you later, but for now, I think you'll enjoy it more if you can think about their faces. It's certainly not going to make things any worse and you have to admit, the Alexis Carrington, June Cleaver, TV-thing wasn't panning out very well at all.

I know I make a difference because I:

A. Have taken up where Mother Teresa left off and am in the process of creating a lasting legacy of hope for the hungry and poor.

B. Started my own religion and am raising my twelve children to spread the word around the world.

C. Am within two weeks of finding a cure for cancer.

D. See the difference I make to people in my regular, old life.

Oprah has said, "I only give money to someone when I know it will have a significant effect on their lives." Here is a woman who could probably donate enough money to have a state re-named after her and yet it's still important to her to make that personal connection. She knows it means more when you see it matter to someone. Well, you might say that's all fine and good for Oprah, but what about the rest of us who can't sin-glehandedly get the country to read more? Where does that leave us?

To be honest with you, when I first realized how important this was to me, my reaction was, oh just great, now on top of everything else I have to do, the only way I'm going to feel good about my life is if I change someone else's. Wonderful, one more thing to add to my list.

But we don't have to do *more*; we can just do it *differently*, or even just *think* about it differently. It doesn't mean accomplishing any more or less than you're doing right now. It just means feeling a lot better about it. I learned this little lesson from an experience with JoAnn.

JoAnn was a big executive, the VP of marketing for a large healthcare company. She will tell you herself, the one thing that she is great at is developing marketing plans and one thing she is terrible at is corporate politics. I personally think that has something to do with having some character, but she continues to see it as a career deficiency.

Well, her company was going through a difficult time and sucking up was being refined into an art form. She was feeling completely unappreciated, so she started interviewing. I think she's brilliant, so it was no surprise to me that she got an offer from another organization for more money. This other organization was even bigger than her company and the job was a perfect fit for her. Plus it paid megabucks. Yet for some reason she had some hesitancy about taking it. In fact, I knew she wanted me to talk her out of it. Far be it from me to talk someone out of taking a pile of money from some big company, so I was determined not to give an opinion. I was going to make her tell me herself why she didn't want to do it.

I asked her what she liked to do the most and how did this new offer fit that? Her answer was, "What I really like to do is be helpful to people." Now I don't know about you but *helpful* isn't the first word that springs to my mind when I think of an officer of a Fortune 500. A home ec teacher maybe, but the vice president of marketing? But helpful she said, so that's what we went with.

How, I asked her, could she be helpful in this new job as compared to her current one? The new job, it seemed, focused on corporate-type issues—developing big-picture plans while in her current position she was often out in the field working with hospitals helping them with their individual plans.

Her take on the situation was, "I guess I really don't want to take it because it would be all corporate work and I hate that. I don't see where that helps anyone at all." Up until this point she had been fairly frustrated with all the politics of her job, but through the course of our conversation she realized that this was just the current atmosphere of the company. Her actual job was to help people do their jobs better and she was really good at it. The only problem was that she hadn't taken the time to notice.

The next time she was out at a hospital she spent the usual two days doing a complete analysis of their numbers and helping them develop a marketing plan. Then, five minutes before she was ready to leave, she simply asked, "Was this helpful to you?" "Oh, yes," they said, "We were so worried about what we were going to do and now you've made it so easy for us. We can't thank you enough, we're going to be so much more effective this year. We don't know what we would have done without you."

FLASH

If you're not sure if it matters, ask!

Suddenly the same work JoAnn had been doing for years was connected to someone and now it mattered, so she mattered. I told you that I didn't want you to do more and I don't. I want to help you find the meaning in what you're already doing.

Don't go telling yourself that getting some feedback on whether it matters isn't important. Mother Nature knows otherwise. She had to make sure we didn't let our brood starve over a dark winter or, heaven forbid, not reach their full potential. Since she couldn't afford to let us go down the wrong path for too long, she wired us to "check" and "check" a lot. After all, the survival of the species is at stake here!

Communication skills weren't exactly the cave kid's forte, so Mother Nature wanted women to constantly look for evidence that all was going OK. If you need some feedback every now and again, it doesn't mean you're hopelessly insecure. It just means you're the sophisticated product of an evolutionary process going back thousands of years.

It's different for the other half of the species. Imagine what would happen if right before they were about to pounce on a big mammoth, Zorg turned to his brothers Ogg and Glug and asked, "So, are you guys OK with how this has been going, because I'd really like some feedback here before we try to bag this one." After the mammoth takes off, poor Zorg will probably end up being the food for the winter while Ogg and Glug exchange a series of wondering grunts about their brother's stupidity. Poor sap, he just didn't get it. You never check, it ruins the hunt.

I was explaining this theory to my friend and ex-coworker Debby and she said, "Oh God, Lisa, that sounds like you're going back to that awful *should list*. I sit in my garage office every day and make telemarketing calls. How is that making a difference or a connection to anyone?"

What Debby failed to realize was that when we worked together, talking to her on the phone was one of the brightest spots of my day. She's a great friend, hysterically funny, and you can count on her for anything. Her work was definitely connected to me and after asking her, it sounds like she matters a great deal to the folks she's working with now. I might also add that making a living for her family ranks pretty high up there in the "connecting our tasks to people" category in my book.

Maybe you are making a difference; you just don't have anyone to point it out to you. Start asking a little more and you might find out. My friend Myra found out without even meaning to.

Myra cleans house for a living and although she's great at it, not many people bother to tell her. Most of her customers work during the day, so she never actually sees them. Last summer Myra decided to take a vacation, so she had to miss a week with several of her regulars. She called them all and for the most part left messages on their machines. One woman called her back. Myra had never actually met her because the husband had hired her and they were never home. Every week Myra just let herself in, worked alone for several hours, and left. The woman always left her a check, but never said anything one way or the other about the job she did. You know what the woman said when she called?

> *"I just want to make sure you're not dropping us. You're not, are you? Because I couldn't stand to lose you. The day you come is the best day of the week. When I walk in and smell that 'Myra's been here smell' I just love it."*

So if you're wondering if what you're doing counts, ask yourself (or better yet them) what they'd do if you quit doing whatever it is you're doing. You'll find out whether it counts or not.

Making a difference is certainly not just about work. If you're volunteering your time, ministering to the poor, or even just being a good neighbor you're probably already getting something back from it. And I would hope someone's pointed it out to all you teachers, nurses, nannies, mommies, counselors, and social workers out there. But in case you missed it: On behalf of the rest of the planet, let me just say thank-you. The entire future of society as we know it is in your hands and yes, it counts. Your halos are in the mail.

For the less noble among us, my friend Teressa says that even making someone's day a little better counts for something. Teressa is the one who doesn't waste her time on housework anymore. She says there's a way to make a difference anywhere, even at Wal-Mart.

> "I'll see some mother in the store whose child is having a tantrum. Everyone's staring at her and I know just how she feels, like they all think she's the worst mother on the planet. I look right at her, smile, and say, 'Well if she's gonna imitate my daughter, she's gonna have to scream a lot louder than that.' Someone did that to me once and it just eased the whole situation. If I can do that for someone, it makes my day."

Teressa went on to tell me that she goes home picturing that woman and her child having a little bit better day because of her. She says,

> "I've lost it with my kids before, everyone has. But if I can prevent that from happening one time, I've helped. That's why I never say, 'Oh, she's tired' or 'poor little thing, it's hard to shop for so long.' Those things sound like they help, but they don't. The mother just feels guilty for dragging her out too long. I want that

woman to know it's not her fault, and it happens to everyone. And if I see one bit of tension go out of her face, I know it worked."

That's all I mean by connecting, looking for that personal connection in some of the things you're already doing. If Teressa can find it and make a difference at Wal-Mart, you can probably find one where you are. She doesn't even need to ask if she's made a difference, she can check by the look on their faces.

If thinking about the faces while you're in the car pool line isn't enough for you, here are two other suggestions:

First, ask about what you're already doing. Oh, I know you shouldn't have to ask, they should be thanking you anyway, but the simple fact is, they're not. Either because they're too wrapped up in their own little worlds, or like Ogg and Glug, they don't realize how much you need to hear it. That's why you might want to start with somebody like a neighbor, teacher, colleague, or friend. Kids, husbands, and bosses tend to be notoriously ungrateful and require some special handling that I'll cover later. Pick somebody easy for this first round. After you've done whatever it is you do, turn to them and simply ask, "Did this make a difference to you?" You might be surprised at what you find out.

If that doesn't work, you could stage a strike to see how much they miss it. But try asking first. Once you've gotten a little feedback on what you already do, it's time to spread a little of that good karma to the rest of the world.

The next time you're waiting in line at a store, and for those of you who don't have a Wal-Mart down the street, the grocery or drugstore work just as well; take a minute to do what Teressa does. Make a connection and make someone's day a little better. I don't care if it's the frazzled mother or a checkout clerk that needs a smile, just do something.

Trust me, it's going to make your day a little better too. And besides, it doesn't take any more time than scanning the tabloids for another Elvis sighting.

CALLING ALL CAMP COUNSELORS

The best times of my life were when I:

A. Could get my cut flowers to last a bit longer, because you never know when someone from *Home, Hearth and Haven* magazine will drop by.

B. Had decent hand servants to peel my grapes. Having to spit those pesky skins out in my pool gets in the way of my tabloid reading.

C. Had twenty-four-hour access to my broker so that I could monitor my financial situation any time of the day or night.

D. Spent my time with a great group of people.

Making a difference to people does a lot for women, but there's another aspect of connecting that can make it even better. A least that's what these women said:

"I guess I was the happiest when I was in my first job. I worked with a group of mostly women and I felt like what we were doing was really important. Looking back, I guess it wasn't really that big a deal, but at the time I felt so excited by it and I loved the people I was working with."

—Donna, healthcare executive

"One of my best times was when my kids were little and we were living on the base. Our husbands were gone all the time, but it really didn't matter because I was in it together with all the other women. Everyone was the same rank and made the same money, which was not much. We would go from house to house with the kids in tow. Everyone pitched in and helped everyone else. I might not have said so at the time, but looking back those really were the happiest days of my life."

—Bonnie, a retired Air Force wife

"As trite as this sounds I was really happy in high school. I lived in a small town and I was a part of everything—choir, the band, National Honor Society, drama. . . . It was really a great time in my life. I was so social, everything revolved around doing things with friends."

—Deb, who still remembers it thirty-five years later

"Everywhere I go around here I see people I know, it just makes me feel so connected and welcome. I'm really the happiest right now because I feel such a part of things."
—Allison, on living in her community

For most women, the best times of our lives were when we shared our time or experiences with other people. You see, it's not just about the people for whom you make a difference; it's the people that make the difference to *you*.

FLASH

Women need to be in relationships; it is essential to the survival of our souls.

I didn't realize just how much I needed those connections until I didn't have them. Besides the birth of my children, surprisingly enough, one of the happiest times of my own life was when I first worked for that small training company. I joined them after a less than scintillating stint in sales with a packaged goods giant, and I loved it. What made it so great at first, as opposed to later on when it had me questioning my purpose in life?

The first clue comes when I think back to the interview. My future boss asked me how I would adjust to working for such a small company after being with the big guys. Before I could even think, I blurted out, "Well, you know, I worked for a really small newspaper in college and to tell you the truth I was happier there." I had not realized it until just that moment, when the words where coming out of my mouth, but it was true! I was happier when I made $65.00 a week working with all my buddies on the college paper.

As for that job with the big guys? **I hardly had any friends at work because they pitted us all against each other. I felt like a nobody, I was a cog for a corporate giant and I hated it!** The only thing I actually liked about that job was how impressed people were when I told them I had it. It took me five years to figure that out!

Well, I jumped ship from the big company and for a while our little company was everything I thought it would be. I felt like my contributions counted and I was connected. Our company was so small that every time we brought in a new client it was a really big deal. And just like in college, I worked with great people and we were all in it together. Come to think of it, that job didn't really quit being great until my boss and most of my friends had left. It became even less great when the president told me to handle all my communication to him through E-mail because it was "more efficient" and it became just a job when I slaved away on a new account and no one, including the customer, noticed.

Why was I dissatisfied? Because if you're disconnected, you forget why you're doing the work. And I don't care whether it's your job or a spa day, it's not as much fun when you do it alone. We can thank our old friend Mother Nature for this one too.

She might have planned for us to be mothers, but she was pretty worried about our ability to pull it off, so she took that wiring one step further. Think about how things got done back then. In addition to raising the cave kids, the women planted, maintained the home fire (literally), and kept the wolves at bay while the men were off hunting. There is no way we could hack it alone or without instruction. Working cooperatively was the only way anything got done.

How else in the world were the inexperienced women going to plant enough food for winter or learn to breast-feed a baby? It doesn't come quite as naturally as you may have been led to believe. They needed to learn from day-to-day involvement with other women and the sharing of information. The more people these women connected with the better likelihood that they and their offspring would survive another winter.

Mother Nature didn't realize that we would invent a nifty concept called the supermarket and be able to rent a video on the womanly art of breast-feeding, but her plan still works. That's why we're the happiest when we have a group of people in it with us. We know it works better that way.

Answer this: What were some of the best times in your life? Were you alone? As you think about this, I don't want you to remember the best *thing* that ever happened to you, but about the happiest period of your life? Your answer may surprise you. I know my friend Laura's did.

It was the first time I'd seen her since she had her second

child, so we had to spend plenty of time trying to understand the exponential math of adding another baby to the mix. You know how one plus one equals five when it comes to children. When I got around to asking about her best time:

"Oh," she said, over the crying baby, "I can tell you right now, I know exactly when I was the happiest. It was the summer after my junior year in college and I was working at a church camp. It was my second summer there and most of the other counselors had come back as well. We all knew each other and just had the best time. Different kids came every few weeks and we really felt great about what we were doing with them. In fact, the reason I remember it so well is that one night walking back to my cabin I had that exact thought, 'This is the happiest I have ever been in my life.' "

Moments later she said,

"I can't believe that was my answer, I'm so embarrassed, that's what I came up with. Here I have a husband I love, a terrific two-year-old and healthy new baby, household help, a great career, and the best time in my life was when I was a camp counselor!!! I feel so ungrateful."

I tell you this story to emphasize it's not what *should* have been the best time, it's what actually was. No one but you is going to know how you answer this.

Now that you've thought about your best time, think about your worst. When did you feel like you didn't count for anything?

JoAnn's first comment was, "If Mother Nature wired us for motherhood, my wiring must have scrambled for a while, because I couldn't stand it to start with." Yes, this wonderful mother who has raised a self-sufficient college graduate, who does volunteer work in his free time, truly cited her son's early years as one of the worst times of her entire life.

She had moved to Arkansas when she was pregnant and because she planned to stay home after the baby was born, she didn't look for a job. They moved because her husband had gotten a new job as a sales rep. He was on the road and cell phones had yet to be invented, so he was basically unreachable. They lived in a neighborhood that wasn't finished yet and everyone that did live there was at work all day.

This was bad enough when she was pregnant, but at least then she could go out and do something. Once she had the baby, things went from bad to worse. Her exact memory is,

"He cried nonstop and I thought I was going to go insane. I couldn't bear it when it was time for my husband to leave in the morning because I knew I was going to be home with this crying baby for ten hours straight. Thank heavens he didn't travel."

Once she found out her son was allergic to milk, she was less miserable, but she also said that she didn't start to feel better until she went back to work part-time when he was three.

Did she feel this way because she's a terrible mother? No. Because he was an awful baby? No. Because the only way a woman can find fulfillment is through work? No. Because she had a burning desire to put on panty hose every day? No. It was simply because she was lonely and she wasn't connected. JoAnn was reluctant to let me use this story because she didn't want her grown son to think she didn't love him.

This is a woman who has devoted every available moment and brainwave she had to raising this young prince and she's worried about the fact that she wasn't in a state of rapture during his early years. She clearly made all the difference in the world to him and in hindsight she's delighted that she spent that period of time in that way. The problem wasn't what she was doing; it was that she was doing it *alone*. She didn't have anybody beside her who knew just what she was going through. After all, her husband had the nerve to go work all day. And there was no one to remind her how important what she was doing was when it got hard.

I convinced her that we had to tell her story because it lets the rest of us know that if you aren't enthralled with your own particular state it doesn't mean you're lazy, unloving, a bad mother, a slack employee, or whatever else you're beating yourself up about.

One of the mistakes a lot of us make is that we assume that

if we're unhappy we've chosen the wrong role for ourselves, when maybe it's just the circumstances we're doing it in. If you're not happy right now it isn't necessarily because you've made a terrible mistake in the way you set up your life. You might not be connected enough. Or maybe you're finding fault with your relationships when the reality is you just don't have enough of them to take full advantage of that wiring.

When you thought of your best and worst times, what was the difference? Was it what you were doing or who you were doing it with? Is there any way you can recapture at least a little of it in the life you've got now?

There aren't any openings at church camp and my old college paper still only pays sixty-five bucks a week, so those options don't look too viable. Let's start with something a little smaller. If we can't go back to the situation, maybe we can just get back to some of the people. I told you at the beginning of this book I think we tend to put ourselves last on our own priority lists, so now here's when I ask you to move yourself up a notch or two.

All I want you to do is reconnect with one or two of those old friends. I know it will take a little time, but remember I earned the right to ask you, since I knocked that perfect thing off your list. You can do this instead of straightening your house or planning a week's worth of dietetic menus.

I'd like you to call or actually see one of those people from your best time. If that's not an option, you can get started with a letter, but eventually I'd like you to have a real conversation.

You deserve the pleasure of talking with a friend that doesn't want or need anything from you except to hear the sound of your voice and know you're OK. Talk about the great times you had back then and why they were so much fun. Find out who they've kept up with and how everyone else is doing. Take the time to listen as well as talk, and I shouldn't have to remind you, but in case you forgot: **Do not under any circumstances be your fake self and trot out that stupid "perfect" thing!** This is as much for the friend as it is for you, so don't blow it with that one.

You'll soon remember just how much those friends can mean in your life. And call me an optimist, but I'm also hoping this puts connecting with them a little higher on your list.

264 EXTRA THOUGHTS

I typically have a lot of deep meaningful conversations with:

A. My soul mate and life partner, because he is the only one who will put aside his own concerns and focus exclusively on what I have to say.

B. My boss, because my organization is passionately committed to my development as a human being not just how much work I can produce.

C. My children, who realize that I am a woman with independent needs and thoughts, not just a servant to do their every bidding.

D. The guy in the paper hat at the other end of the drive-through speaker.

A few of you may be thinking it's a good thing I'm married or have kids because those are my connections. I hate to tell you but even Olivia Walton probably needed a little more. As I seem to recall, John Boy did eventually go off to college.

But when you have that first baby, it's hard to imagine you could ever need anyone else. It doesn't matter if it was fifty days or fifty years ago, for a lot of us it was just magic.

If you don't have any children, or you do and your memory of that time was a sleepless nightmare (my second child), believe me I'm not saying babies are the key to happiness. But most women find motherhood a life-defining event and there are some reasons why that applies to all of us, whether you're done with it, have yet to do it, or never got around to doing it at all.

Motherhood is the first time we are in a relationship that is just about the relationship. There are no hidden agendas, no past hurts, no insecurities, just two people that exist solely for each other.

My own mother once told me long before I had children, "Nobody loves you like a baby." I remember thinking, "What the hell is she talking about?" As the oldest of four, my experience with babies was that they were crying, eating, slobbering, pooping blobs that demanded twenty-four hours a day and who never said thank-you.

That's everyone else's baby. Your own baby, of course, has achieved a new emotional plane unbeknownst to other lesser babies, because your baby loves *you*. I think what my mother meant was, that this is the only time in your life when someone will love you just because you exist. You don't have to do anything, say anything, be perfect, peppy, or anything else. Come to think of it, there is one other person that gets loved like that, and that's of course the baby.

Many women find this time so fulfilling because they are connected in a way like never before: They're a part of something, they mean something. In fact, to the baby they mean everything. And that's what Mother Nature had in mind.

As a mother, you must connect to all of your children all the time. In the beginning the need to connect is so strong, some of us cannot physically bear to let the child out of our arms for a moment, much less out of our sight. I know I couldn't.

I remember Christmas dinner, right after we brought our first baby girl home. We were all sitting at the table and my husband had put our four-day-old daughter on the floor beside him in an infant seat where she lay comfortably asleep. This stable, government-approved, presanitized-by-yours-truly, seat was unfortunately out of my line of sight. I calmly suggested to him that perhaps we could move the seat so that I could keep an eye on her. His most "helpful" response? "She's fine, I'll watch her, you just enjoy your meal."

Well, I had sworn that I was never going to be one of those ridiculous women who won't let anyone else including their husbands touch the baby. I had lots of experience with babies, remember? I knew that I would have no problem letting my husband take care of her, that's what he *should* be doing, right? He had even taken a class in infant care. We were in this thing together.

Yet, here I sat at Christmas dinner, craning my neck like a scene from *The Exorcist* trying to get a glimpse of a fast-asleep baby not two feet away. My dad, an experienced father of four, had the good sense to intervene. "Son," he asked, "do you remember hunting with your father when you were growing up? You know that rule about not getting between the mother and the cub? Well, guess what, buddy? You're there, and I suggest you move before she bites your arm off!"

We were laughing about it later that week and my younger brother, who was single with no children at the time, said in an amazing moment of insight, "You know it really makes sense that you don't want to put the baby down, even for a second. If you laid your baby down a couple of hundred years ago, she might be eaten by some animal." He was exactly right. I wasn't insane, my thinking did defy all logic, but that's because it wasn't thinking at all, it was instinct.

I bring that story up as an example of how powerful the connection urges are. Throughout the lives of their children, mothers must focus on every nuance of their behavior, learn their expressions, their different cries and connect with them so well that they can tell when they're sick even before they know it themselves.

We crave those close, intimate relationships you read about in romance novels, where they're soul mates and can read each other's thoughts. Mother Nature may not have been up to speed on Danielle Steele, but she knew enough to make sure that need was right up there with chocolate for most of us.

She also knew that the survival of the species was dependent on us having more than one child. So it is completely unrealistic to think that she gave us connection wiring that will ever be satisfied with just one or two connections. After all, given the perils that awaited the average human back then and the lack of well-baby care, Mother Nature wanted to make sure we all popped out at least a half a dozen bambinos just for the species to break even.

Once again she wires us for a job and completely ignores the fact that we won't all do the job and that doing the job well means you eventually work yourself out of it. Of course, in her original plan those of us who made it through childbirth alive, died about the time we finished procreating. What did she care what we did with the wiring once her part was done?

FLASH

You've got the baby wiring for a lifetime, the baby only needs it for a few years.

So whether you have ten or none, as JoAnn can tell you, they will all eventually have the nerve to grow up, leave, and get a life of their own. So there you'll be, wiring in place and nothing to do with it.

Think a man can fill it up? I wouldn't count on that one. Mother Nature couldn't afford to give them that soul-mate wiring; after all, men had to go off and hunt for weeks at a time. But let me share with you a little scientific fact I ran across lately: It has been proven that the average man thinks about sex at least once every five minutes, while the average woman thinks about it once an hour.

My first reaction was, How do men get *anything* done? My next thought was, Who are these women? Are any of them over twenty? Once an hour? Try once a week. But I've asked around, and in a random survey of my own, the numbers hold up. Even my own husband said the every five minutes thing sounded "about right." No wonder he can't get home from work on time if he has to interrupt his job every five minutes for that!

Let's do a little math. Start with the premise men and women have the exact same number of thoughts in a given day. And let's say that we both want to share about 50 percent of what's on our minds with someone else. If you are counting on one man to fill this need for you, I feel obligated to inform you that you will be left with 264 more thoughts to share at the end of each and every twenty-four hour period, because while you were pondering the current political landscape, he was thinking about sex.

And that's just after one day. The prospects for an actual relationship look even more bleak. If you multiply those 264 extra thoughts by the 365 days in a year, you will get 96,360 extra thoughts. It just keeps adding up. If you're lucky enough to be in a long-term marriage, by the time you reach your silver anniversary you will have had 2,409,000 extra thoughts.

I think it's pretty obvious here, you're gonna have to have some friends to share those thoughts with. I suggest making sure a lot of them are women. Because besides the fact that they are spending a hugely disproportionate amount of their time thinking about sex, I've also noticed that men tend to use the seesaw method of conversation any time we start talking about ourselves.

For example, in my author bio I say I have a job, kids, laundry, and so on. My brother read it and said I made it sound like my husband wasn't doing anything. I look at it and don't see where I said one word about what he was or wasn't doing. For all anyone knows he teaches our children how to build houses for the homeless every second he's not supporting our family. The comment was about me, not him. But apparently men don't see it that way. If I say I'm doing this, it must mean you're not. We both can't be at the same level. For one to be up, the other must be down. Thus the seesaw.

If you think the man in your life is any different, why don't you try complaining to him about all your responsibilities and everything you have to do and then see just how long you can go before he gets defensive and interrupts with, "Well, what do you want me to do about it? I've got a ton of stuff on my list too you know, and I'm doing the best I can here." My friend Rachelle got to ten minutes, but she had only been engaged for two weeks at the time, so I'm not sure it counts.

Oh, I know, I know, Mr. *Men are from Mars* John Gray says it's because they love you so much they want to jump in and fix everything for you. Maybe. Or maybe it's because they can't fathom that absolutely everything you say doesn't have something to do with them. When it might actually be about *you*. Call me a cynic, but the only people I've ever met that could grasp that concept were women and highly paid therapists.

I love my sweet husband dearly, he's been there for me in every way possible, and he's a great father to our girls. But the simple fact is men aren't programmed like us and if we keep looking to them to fill all our needs we're going to wind up so frustrated that the one time a week our thoughts actually do match theirs we'll be too mad to do anything about it.

I'm no counselor, but I suspect one of the problems with a lot of marriages is that quite frankly, we're expecting just a little too much communication from them. Think about it. Back in the old days—the cave or the '50s, your choice—the women all hung around together raising the kids and had a chance to talk. If there was anything to discuss, they'd already dissected it six ways to Sunday before the men got home. Men got the abbreviated version and that's just how they liked it. My informal research tells me they haven't changed.

There you have it, the kids grow up and the men are off in a fog about you-know-what all the time, so we better start looking for some other connections. Some of you may be already doing it, but for a lot of us it's a little harder than it sounds.

LIFE OF THE PARTY

If someone tells me they don't want to go to a party I think they are

A. Shy and must not have a lot of confidence.

B. Snobby and think they're better than everyone else.

C. Socially inept.

D. Perfectly normal and need some alone-time to reenergize themselves.

Before we talk any more about connecting with people, let me just say that I know it comes a little bit more naturally to some people than others. I'd like to share some facts about the difference between introverts and extroverts. When most people think of those two words they think of the difference between the woman with the lampshade on her head wowing the crowd with a rip-roaring joke and some poor thing standing at the back of the room trying to blend into the wallpaper. That's not it at all. There's been a lot of actual scientific research on the subject and it boils down to this. Extroverts get their energy from other people and introverts get it from being alone.

FLASH

It's not about your social skills, it's about how you recharge your batteries.

Obviously there is no right way to be. But I will also tell you that current research estimates that extroverts represent about 75% of the population and introverts are 25%. If you ask me, introverts have gotten a completely bad rap because of it. There is absolutely nothing wrong with needing some time alone to reenergize yourself. The problem is our society won't let you take it.

In fact, some researchers believe it's closer to a 50/50 split, but our predisposition to extroverts is forcing a huge number of introverts to deny their natural instincts and move to the other side. I can only guess what Mother Nature thinks about that.

Perhaps we should call her Mistress of the Obvious, because she knew that whole talker/listener thing works better with representation from each side. She had a number of agendas going on so she wanted to make sure that both the hunters and the gatherers had a good mix. You'll never bring in the harvest or bag the boar if everyone in the group has to be center stage. And you certainly can't organize an effort if nobody wants to bark out the orders.

Never one just to live in the moment, Mother Nature was looking out for the future as well. And a continual supply of cave kids was a pretty pivotal part of the plan. You know that old expression "opposites attract"? Well, hunting and gathering aren't the only projects that work better with someone from each side. People didn't bathe back then, and she had to find some way to get the sparks to fly.

Her brilliant solution was an even introvert/extrovert split for each sex. The work gets done and then we can all pair off accordingly. It's a fairly logical plan and I'm sure she is completely flabbergasted as to how we got so confused about it.

How does this influence making connections? Well, for starters you need to figure out which one you are. There's a whole battery of shrink tests you can take, but it's usually pretty easy to figure out.

If you go to a party and talk with a bunch of people do you have more energy or less when you're done? Once you factor out too much to drink, boring people, and the act of balancing a glass and a plate while standing, you probably know the answer. Again the key here is not whether you *can* connect with other people, it's how much it takes out of you when you do. On the flip side, if you're spending the day alone, is a call from a friend a welcome distraction or an uninvited interruption? It may vary depending on how tired you are—everyone needs a little time alone—but generally speaking, extroverts feed off other people and introverts feel like they're being fed off of.

The difficulty is that introverts still need connections. You might not need as many and, yes, it's going to take more effort on your part to make them, but they're still an important key to happiness. At least according to my cousin Emily,

> *"You know I've always been the kind of person that liked to be alone, something nobody in my family understands. My job requires that I interact with people all day long and then when I get home, I've got the kids. Sometimes I just want to crawl into a quiet hole. I haven't really kept up with my friends because it was always so much work, but now I've got a problem and I'd really like to talk it through with someone. If I called one of them, I would have to explain the whole thing from scratch."*

As much as the "quiet hole" beckons, you're still going to be better off if you have some relationships. There are a few things you can do to make it a little easier for both sides of the equation.

For the introverts: First, make sure you have enough time alone. This might seem like contradictory advice, but trust me you'll never have the energy to make any connections unless you give yourself some downtime to gather your strength. I would hope I've helped you slash enough items off your *should list* to make room for this time.

The next step is to lighten up on yourself. Everyone doesn't expect you to be the life of the party. All those extroverts are more than happy to play that role and they need an audience to pull it off. Don't waste a whole lot of time worrying about how you're going to fill up the conversation. Remember, whenever you meet someone new, it's three to one odds that they're an extrovert. Getting a word in edgewise will probably be more of a problem than some awful moment of silence.

Another thing to keep in mind is that smaller numbers will probably work better for you. If you have a choice, don't tackle a big group, start with three or four people. Be sure it's large enough so you don't have to do all the talking, but small enough so that you can make some real connections.

Because interacting with people is going to take energy away from you, I also suggest you be fairly selective on where you spend it. If you let your job, husband, and kids sap you of every bit you've put yourself last on your own list again. Those people might be where you spend a lot of your energy, but try to save a little for some other connections. The next time they start sucking you dry, send them to a party and curl up with a good book. You'll all be more energized when you're done.

Which brings me to my suggestions for extroverts. Hopefully you read the above and you now know that although you're in the majority, everyone is not like you. If you live with, gave birth to, or work with someone from the other side, don't take it personally. They need their time alone just as much as you need to be around others. Give them a break and go feed off your own kind for a while.

You also need to realize that initiating conversations isn't everyone's forte. So the next time you meet someone new, don't mistake shyness for snottiness. It doesn't mean they aren't worth getting to know. Some people just take more time to open up, so be patient. You've got a vested interest here because having people in your life is an absolute necessity if you're an extrovert.

It's no coincidence that solitary confinement is an effective discipline technique for toddlers and hardened criminals. When you get your energy from others, too much alone time lets your reserves run down, and brief little interactions with acquaintances won't be enough to fill it back up.

A two- or three-minute chat, or a number of relationships where you do all the work aren't enough for anyone, let alone an extrovert. You'll never get that, "I'm a part of something" feeling from those. You need some of those *real-self* relationships.

You don't have to live your life surrounded by a cast of thousands. But no matter which side of the introvert/extrovert scale you fall on, you do deserve to have some people in your life you can really count on.

THE BEST-LAID PLANS

Mother Nature had a plan: We would work collectively, connecting with the cave kids and each other, check a lot, and know we made a difference every time we all lived to see the dawn of a new day. Great. What are we supposed to do in today's world? I know, let's all chuck our lives, go live on some commune, and spend our days gathering nuts for the winter with all the other earth mothers. Sign up if you want, but a week without a shower and no credit cards isn't a program I can muster up a lot of enthusiasm for.

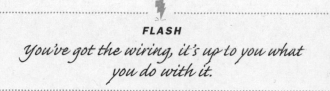

FLASH

You've got the wiring, it's up to you what you do with it.

Mother Nature was concerned about survival, not happiness in the modern world. Keep in mind, she also planned for breasts to be functional feeding items that deflate upon use and gave us hips meant for carrying around twenty extra pounds in case of famine. And persistent soul that she is, she doesn't show any sign of letting up on that plan either. The sooner we make peace with her agenda, the happier we'll be.

I said before, I don't want you to have to change your life. I just want to help you change the way you feel about it. You don't have to sign up for the commune. If you want to connect and make a difference to people, you can do that in the life you've already got. Society's gotten us pretty far off course by putting this perfect thing and a host of other obstacles in our way. Let's see if there are a few places where we can get back on track.

CHAPTER FOUR

Is Anybody Out There?

"Loneliness and the feeling of being unwanted is the most terrible poverty."

—Mother Teresa

WHAT WAS YOUR NAME AGAIN?

Whenever I interact with someone my first thought is:

A. Wow, another opportunity to connect with a human being.

B. I wonder how can I make a difference in this person's life?

C. I sure hope this broadens my perspective on the human race.

D. How long is this going to take?

Women may define themselves through relationships, but you sure wouldn't know it from looking at our lives. At least that's what my research had to say:

"I've gotten to where I'm reluctant to even get involved in the neighborhood or the school. I mean why bother, we're probably just going to move in two years anyway."

—Cathy, on being relocated five times in ten years of marriage

"Our company just put us through this big team-building exercise, what a joke. Everyone knows they rank us against each other before they give out raises. Like I'm going to bond with my competition."

—Maddie, after her latest sales meeting

"When I was growing up all the moms got together for coffee every afternoon while the kids played outside. Now all the other moms I know just wave at each other in carpool line."

—Tricia, referring to the neighborhood she grew up in

"I get fifty E-mails a day and every single one of them is from someone that needs something right now. I can't remember the last time someone asked how I was doing."

—Tracy, on her daily "connections"

"Who has time to stop and talk with anyone? What with the kids and my job, it's all I can do to keep my head on straight. The last thing I'm going to do is engage in some mindless chitchat when I've got a million other things to do."

—Debby, on why she doesn't make the effort with her neighbors

"How can I open up and be my real self at work? I'm the boss for heaven's sake. What with the hours I put in and the travel, it's a wonder I find the time to call my own mother. The one that knows the most about my life right now is probably my hair-dresser."

—Donna, discussing how hard it is to find friends

"Friends, what are those? The last time I saw friends every day was when I was in high school."

—Deb, on her current social life

Since when did people fall off our to-do list? Oh, there are still the kids, the boss, the husbands. They all make it to the list because they usually want something from us and they're not shy about asking. But it's shocking how little time we spend on any other relationships. And I think it's affecting us more than we even realize.

For starters, it's pretty easy to succumb to the pursuit of perfection when you're denied access to real people who might show you anything different. Let's be honest here—don't you measure your own life by using other people as a comparison? I know we're not supposed to, but we all do it. Don't give me that tired old line about "don't worry about what your neighbor is doing, just focus on just doing the best *you* can." Yeah, yeah, yeah, that may be fine advice if you're working on a Girl Scout craft; but how else are you supposed to figure out if you're normal or not unless you have some sort of benchmark?

The problem is that most of us don't see enough of the details of others' real lives to get an accurate reading. Think about it, which friends do you know more about? Rachael and Ross and the gang at the coffee shop on Thursday nights or your next-door neighbors? Face it, nobody's life stacks up very well against a bunch of skinny, highly-paid actors.

I might also point out that while you may enjoy getting to know them, the friends on TV couldn't give a flip about what's going on in your life. Which brings me to an even worse problem this disconnectedness creates—loneliness.

Lonely might not seem like the right word to describe our hectic lives. In fact you might be thinking, "Lonely, she must be kidding. My biggest problem is that I can't *get* a moment alone. The phone is ringing off the hook, I've got a line of people outside my office, and my kids won't even let me go to the bathroom by myself." It might seem like the last thing you need in your life is more people, but let me ask you this: How many of those people are real friends? I don't mean friendly acquaintances, I mean *friends,* the kind you can really count on.

Who do you know who would patiently listen while you talk through a problem you're having with your kids or your boss? How many people would support you if you were going through a bad time? Who could you call up in the middle of the night and ask to drop everything and come tend to your crisis with no questions asked? And here's the kicker: Who do you think would stand up at your funeral and talk about what a difference you made in their life?

You may have a list as long as your arm, but if you're like a lot of us, half your own family doesn't even meet that criteria.

FLASH

*Acquaintances aren't enough,
we need real friends.*

If the world stopped and you fell off, an acquaintance might look up, a friend would really care.

If you don't have enough friends in your life right now, don't beat yourself up about it. You're not the only one and it's hardly your fault. We've been disconnected everywhere, from our neighborhoods, to our cars, to the voice mail hell we endure every time we try to get a live person on the phone. Society has set up so many obstacles for us it's a miracle any of us even know each others' names. So if you don't have enough connections in your life right now, it's not because you aren't a perfectly delightful person that others would love to spend more time with. It's because the rest of the world has been working against you.

What can we do about it? Well, the good news is we're all in the same boat. The bad news is, it's going to take some actual work to get out of it. Not a lot, but some.

Earlier in this book I asked you to connect and make a difference to the lady at Wal-Mart. I'm hoping that you did it. It's easy and can make your day. Now I'm going to ask you to take

it a step further and invest some time in a few more long-term 105
relationships. I think you'll find this does more than just make
your day, it makes your life.

WESTWARD HO!

**Whenever I want to connect with people in a meaningful
way I:**

**A. Simply step outside my door where I'm surrounded by
friendly neighbors eager to reminisce about our latest block
party.**

**B. Call up my boss because he's always eager for a long talk
about the meaning of life.**

**C. Go on the Internet because I know that you can find real
people being their real selves in a chat room.**

**D. Turn on Nick at Nite and drop in on the bar where "every-
body knows your name and they're always glad you came."**

There's a lot of talk these days about the lack of community
in our lives. But let's look at the root of the problem during the
years before the virtual office.

Think about how this country was founded. A group of people left their extended family, friends, their entire lives and got
on boats that may or may not have known where they were
going and went to a land where they had no idea what awaited

them. Whose idea was this? I can tell you one thing, it was not the women's! What woman is going to leave all her friends and everything that she knows behind, to sit in cramped quarters for months, only to end up having to replant a garden she already had going pretty well back in the homeland?

Move ahead a bit and think about how our country expanded—the new frontier, manifest destiny, and so on. It seems like every time someone wanted to pursue the American Dream they were required to strike off for a different part of America to do it. The forces of society have tried to disconnect us since the first boat hit the water. Today's forces are working even harder against you if you do try to connect.

We live in one place, yet work in another. Most of our mail is addressed to occupant. Neighbors move in and out like a revolving door. Half our waking hours are spent in automobiles or other forms of transportation. The technology that's supposed to keep us "in touch" has replaced live conversations altogether. How can we feel we make a difference to anyone when most of the people we interact with don't even know our names?

It wasn't always that way. Somewhere between the new frontier and the Net I understand there were things called neighborhoods and towns. Some of you may still live in one, but for the rest of us, here's the way they worked: Everyone pretty much lived and worked in the same community, your family was close by, and everywhere you went someone knew who you were.

I doubt it was Nirvana. If it was, no one would have ever

left. My friend Steve said that in his small Missouri town whenever someone left for the big, wide world it was called, "gettin' over the wall." People left because there might not have been enough privacy, economic opportunity, or shopping malls, but there's still a big advantage to those small communities: People really know you.

There's no way you can go around acting like you're perfect if everyone in town knows you wet your pants in the third grade pageant and your cousin had to take you to the prom. You couldn't go repositioning yourself every time you turned around when your friends, neighbors, customers, and coworkers were all the same people. They were witness to every stupid mistake and problem you ever had. Fortunately once everybody "knew your business," they kept right on interacting with you anyway. And what's more, some of us made the best friends of our lives in those small towns and neighborhoods.

FLASH
Nobody's perfect in a real relationship.

I would hope you've dumped that perfect nonsense by now, but in case you haven't, I feel obligated to inform you it's standing in the way of any real relationships you might have.

For starters, perfection tends to be a rather solitary effort that leaves you with little time or energy for anything else. Beyond just wearing you out, how can you expect anyone to really know you if you continue to present your fake self to the world? There's no way you can connect with people if you're always worried about the impression you're making.

But there's an even more insidious way we get into trouble with the perfect thing. Besides just measuring ourselves against some impossible standard, a lot of us insist on applying it to everyone else too. It's bad enough we beat ourselves up when our lives don't match our little picture, but then we make it worse by discounting anyone else that doesn't measure up to it either.

The irony of this situation is that people's imperfections are what usually bonds us the most. In fact, opening ourselves up to other people is the key to losing the perfect thing. Once you quit being your fake self and give everyone else permission to do the same, you can start some real relationships.

It wasn't our idea to get so disconnected, any more than it was our idea to leave the village and get on those boats. But it happened then and it's happened now. We've let voice mails, sound bites, and TV images replace real people. And the hole it left in our lives is where the perfect thing crept in. It's no surprise we keep expecting everyone to adhere to it. It's all we ever get exposed to.

You can't have a real relationship with those fake images, and if you really want to make a difference to people, do you think it makes a whole lot of sense to start with the perfect ones?

This anonymous world's made it difficult for us to connect,

so don't go making it harder. In the spirit of less work and not more, here's one thing you can strike off your list: Quit worrying about whether everybody else measures up to your standards. The people around you are going to persist in being their imperfect selves whether you like it or not.

Remember, those friends on TV may seem to be a whole lot more interesting than real people, but there's a team of highly paid writers making sure they are. The people in your life didn't get a script. They're wingin' it just like you are.

So let the gang at the coffee shop wait until your next bout with the flu and go for connecting with some live bodies. There's lots of places to find them, but you're going to have to look, and you may have to look hard.

HOME ON THE RANGE

I chose my current home because:

A. My friends and I worked long and hard to build a front-porch community so we can chat all day while we watch our children play happily in the sun.

B. It's directly across the street from the town square and it makes me feel so connected with the hustle and bustle of life happening all around me.

C. I love living in a quaint little cottage with neighbors and friends just an arm's reach away.

D. I could afford it.

Nowhere is being disconnected worse than in where we live. We may not be alone on the prairie, but there are enough actual physical barriers in place to make us feel like we are.

Look at the way our neighborhoods are laid out. JoAnn and I both live in suburbia and we have noticed that it is entirely possible to live for several years in the same home and never actually meet one single person including your next-door neighbors. Why? Because the people that develop subdivisions have, up until recently, been of the stake-your-claim mentality, not of the connections way of thinking.

First of all, just looking at my own neighborhood, the houses are literally unconnected. There are no sidewalks. To get to anyone else's house you must walk into the street. There are also no front porches. All the living is done behind the house where no one can see you at all if you have the highly coveted suburban privacy fence that is the modern version of a moat. It just shouts, "This is my land, trespass if you dare!" It must be pretty important to have one because I had trouble getting anything less in a fence.

My house is on a corner so my backyard is right next to the street. We decided that we wanted to put up a fence. Well, the fence guy comes out and while I am in the process of explaining to him that I would like a low picket fence, he keeps interrupting me. Obviously I must not understand. "People will still be able to see in from the street," he says. "Whatcha' need is one of them six-foot-tall privacy fences." "No," I explain to him, "here is a picture of a white picket fence exactly like what I want." "But lady don't you understand, it's not going to be any cheaper because the lumber comes precut. For the same money I really can build you a much higher fence, it will be much better."

In my subdivision the streets don't really go anywhere and so everyone on the street is either a neighbor or coming to visit a neighbor. Even though we don't have sidewalks, people occasionally walk in the neighborhood. What this gentleman failed to understand was that I actually wanted people to see us and, heaven forbid, say hello. If you've ever gone out into your yard and played with your children for any extended period of time, you realize that you will probably tire of it before they do. Dare I say it, you may even get bored. So, if I had followed this well-meaning fellow's advice, there I would be in the yard, bored without even the hope that someone would walk by and say hello, because we would be, for all practical purposes, alone and completely unconnected. And they wonder why we lose it with the kids sometimes.

Besides, I am a thirty-seven-year-old mother of two children living in the suburbs; what could I possibly be doing in my backyard that I want to keep from the prying eyes of others? The last time I checked, my house had a door and drapes. If I really want to do something immoral or illegal, I would hope I would have the good sense to do it inside.

Now look at garages and their door openers. I don't know about you, but I am too lazy to get out of the car to open and close my garage door every time I go in and out. My parents were too lazy too but they didn't have a handy little gadget, they just left the garage door open all the time. On occasion they actually made eye contact with their neighbors when they got in and out of the car. Now that I think of it, we had so much junk, we left the cars in the driveway and used the garage for storage. No wonder we knew everyone that lived around us.

If you're like most of us your home is also probably a bit bigger than the one you grew up in. On the face of it this seems like a huge improvement. Believe me, sharing a bedroom with a toddler during my teen years is not high on the list of beautiful childhood memories I want to re-create for my own kids. But there's also a downside. When everyone's got their own private space inside the house, they never need to leave it.

If you grew up like I did, Mom was always shoving the kids outside or escaping there herself. Everyone couldn't fit comfortably inside the house, so some of the people actually conducted a large portion of their lives outside it, interacting with the rest of the world.

Even if Mom had tolerated the kids underfoot, I doubt we would have lasted too long. My memories of our indoor options were a small, three-channel TV, a couple decks of cards, a Monopoly game, and a phone we were limited to using in one-minute increments. My parents better have known who the neighbors were. How else could they have ever found us? Nowadays, if you want to track down your kids you'll find them plugged into their phone, computer, Game Boy, or Nintendo.

Sometimes it's not more house that disconnects us, but more land. Those of you living a rural life know exactly what I'm talking about here. Who needs a six-foot-high fence when a few acres guarantees you all the privacy you want? Life in the country sounds like a peaceful escape from the pressures of the daily grind, but how are you supposed to connect with people if it takes a fifteen-minute drive to find any?

I've known a few families that chose this route and it seems like it's usually the man who's the most enamored with it. My own husband says there's something really macho about owning a big spread. "Land is the most tangible asset you can have," he says. "It's more permanent than money in the bank." The fact that it's visible to all your friends helps too. Whipping out your bankbook for guests is a little more awkward.

The 'burbs and prairie pose physical barriers to connecting, but city life has its own obstructions. People may take some initiative to meet each other in a neighborhood, but if you live in a high-rise or apartment building, don't hold your breath. Suburban neighborhoods are often forced to interact to keep the community running, get up the Christmas decorations, keep the common grass mowed, and whatnot. But in an apartment, those responsibilities fall to the others. Think the entrance is looking shabby? No need to call a homeowner's meeting, make your complaint to the building manager.

It's pretty hard to muster up much community spirit when your community consists of thousands of strangers whizzing by in cars and on bikes, or walking hurriedly with a cell phone in their ear. When you're surrounded by so many people, it's almost impossible to narrow it down to just a few. My friend Teri lives in a New York apartment and she says, "I only know two other couples in my building. And the only reason I met them is because they're always out smoking in the stairwell." Guess I've watched one too many *Seinfeld* episodes. I thought life in the city meant laughing it up at the corner diner every other night. Those who live there say it's more of an "every man for himself" mentality. Say hello to a stranger in some cities and the best you'll get is a sideways glance while they try to figure out if you're a tourist or a serial killer.

Once you combine all those physical and social barriers with the fact that we have to get in our cars to go absolutely anywhere, it's no wonder a lot of us live amongst strangers. Some of you may reside in a wonderful small town, where all the houses are off the town square and your family's storefront business has it's own float in the Fourth of July parade. If you do, I'm jealous, but for the rest of us our communities aren't the havens of connectedness they could be.

Our surroundings have changed and so have our lifestyles. I doubt we're going to re-create Cleaver Land in this century. And I'm not so sure I even want to. My friend Ann says, "Oh please, like I'm going to go out and buddy up with some stranger down the street. I've got good friends I haven't seen in months. If I had time for a social life it would be with them."

I realize that my parents actually complained about a lot of the neighbors. And we didn't come up with those block-long hide-and-seek games because we knew young children needed exercise. We were bored! Mom wasn't grand friends with the neighbors because they were so intellectually stimulating. She didn't know anyone else! Hell, half the moms in my old neighborhood didn't even have a car. They couldn't go anywhere else even if they wanted to.

If you've got loads of friends on the other side of town you spend plenty of time with, great. But just because we're not forced into it anymore doesn't mean there isn't still some value in having at least a few of those neighborhood connections. That's what JoAnn found out.

She moved a few years back. Her son was already grown and so it was just her and her husband. They chose a house that was close to both their offices and right near the heart of the city. It was on a nice little street off a main thoroughfare with about fifteen houses on it. JoAnn had her big VP job and was traveling all the time, and her husband had a pretty hectic schedule as well. On weekends they liked to go visit their son, work in the yard, or go antiquing. They came and went in their cars, waving and nodding to the neighbors along the way. All in all, they had a really nice life.

And then came the tornado. It was the worst one they'd ever had and it ripped right through JoAnn's neighborhood. According to her, being in one is a lot different than watching one in the movies:

> *"The noise was deafening, it sounded like the whole house was screaming. I ran down to the basement just as all the power went*

out. I kept shouting for my husband, but I couldn't see or hear a thing. It sounded like the house was being ripped apart right over my head. I've never been more scared in my life."

Well, she lived through it and so did all of her neighbors. Once it was over, everyone went outside to survey the damage. Roofs were torn off, power lines were down, trees were on top of houses, and windows were broken everywhere, but everyone was OK. The entire neighborhood congregated in the middle of the street to wait for help.

JoAnn didn't find her soul mate that night, but she did get to know the people around her a little bit better. As she says, "There's not a whole lot of pretense when you're wearing your pajamas at two in the morning."

From then on it was more than a wave and a nod, sometimes it was an actual conversation. And when a police car was parked outside the woman down the street's house? JoAnn says,

"I was so worried something had happened to her. Here's some-one I didn't even know a few months ago and now I'm ready to break down her door to make sure she's OK. I called her house the second the car drove away. While I was on the phone with her, three other neighbors beeped in."

It turns out the woman had to give a report for something that had happened at work. I suspect if this happened before the tornado, the neighbors would have assumed the worst and dinnertime gossip would have been wondering what kind of

trouble the lady down the block was in. I doubt anyone would have called to find out what really happened.

FLASH

When people don't know you, they're a lot less likely to help you.

Think about it, what do you want people to think if you run outside screaming?

That strange woman looks like a serial killer—lock the door.

Or

That's my neighbor—I better go help her.

They may be boring, loud, nosy, and put inappropriate objects in their front yards, but your neighbors have a big advantage over everybody else. They're there. It doesn't matter whether you live in a country club, apartment building, or trailer park, your neighbors are going to witness the comings and goings in your life whether you like it not. They're also the only ones that can be at your house in two seconds flat, or notice if your four-year-old wanders out into the street. You're going to feel a lot more connected if you know who they are.

Besides making your life a little safer, it just feels better to know the people around you. If you'd like to achieve that "I'm a part of something" feeling, isn't your own neighborhood a good place to get it? I've also found it can take some of the pressure off family life. If you ever need to escape, the friendly face across the street is a lot more accessible than your shrink. It's amazing how many things I need to borrow when my in-laws visit.

I know you didn't choose the neighbors. But I'm also guessing some of your best friends from childhood had more to do with their proximity to your house than your ability to scope out an ideological match at such an early age. So before you get up on some high horse about what's wrong with them and how you have nothing in common, let me remind you: We're looking for a way out of this disconnected mess, lofty standards will only keep you in it.

I hate to point out the obvious here, but the fact that you chose to live in the same place they did might mean you have more in common than you think. So don't wait for a natural disaster, figure out whatever the commonality is—the beach, the schools, or the same boring highway you drive every day to work—and use it as a starting point.

If you're really ambitious and feel motivated to plan a block party or a holiday open house, go for it. But before you do, keep in mind, it's about connecting, not perfection. Save the "Martha Moment" for a bridal shower.

Remember, becoming a little friendlier with one or two of the folks around you can make a difference. The next time you see one of your neighbors, come on out of your house, open up your garage door, leap over your privacy fence, and say hello. It's not going to kill you. There's a really interesting woman inside your house. There might be one down the street too.

HELLO, MY NAME IS

I live in an area where:

A. My family homesteaded generations ago and named a town after itself.

B. I am a pillar of the community and consulted on all civic affairs.

C. Everybody has known and liked me since I was in grade school, so naturally, I'm welcome everywhere I go.

D. I could find a job.

As if our lives weren't difficult enough, a lot of us make matters worse by picking them up and moving every few years. The modern-day Ingalls family might not be able to strike off for the prairie, but they can still uproot their entire lives every year in search of new horizons. We just call it a transfer now. If you've ever had to face this one, you know how tough it can be. Especially if it wasn't your idea.

As my friend Renae said,

"I'm up to my ears in boxes. I've got to get the house organized, keep the kids' spirits up, and find a baseball team that will still take a new player halfway through the season. I'm supposed to be some rah-rah cheerleader for the whole family when I didn't want to move in the first place. His life stays the same. He's got all his buddies and goes to work everyday. I'm the one that has to start all over again."

.... ⚡ ....

FLASH

*The quicker you get connected,
the easier it will be.*

....

A move is hard on everyone, but I think it's the hardest for women. It doesn't matter whether it was your plan or his, the woman is still the one to set up the house and get the family up and running. If that's not enough of a job in itself, it's also the women who usually run the family's social life. I hate to be the bearer of bad news here, but the only way you're going to have one is if you look for it.

I promised not to add to your list unless I took something off, so let me tell you that I am living testament to the fact that a family can live indefinitely with unpacked boxes in the basement and nothing bad happens. Look for friends, not the fine china. And don't go making it harder on yourself before you move in.

I've witnessed a few buyings and sellings in my neighborhood, and I think some of you might be shooting yourself in the foot without even realizing it. If you're buying a house or negotiating a lease, keep in mind that the seller you're being so aggressive with is reporting back every little detail to the neighbors. A family in my neighborhood just sold their house and through the course of the negotiations their widely broadcasted opinion of the buyers went from, "Seems like a nice couple," to, "Those nitpicky vultures who are bleeding us dry." I'm not saying you shouldn't make the best deal you can, but you probably want to think twice before you ask them to surgically remove the oil stains from the driveway. Keep in mind, the welcome-wagon lady is a little busy these days, and it might be awhile before she gets to you.

Remember when you were little and a new family moved into your neighborhood or a new kid showed up at school? It was really a big deal because it only happened once in a blue moon. Now corporate America is sending people to and fro like they're FedEx packages. We've gotten so oblivious to it that when a FOR SALE sign pops up, all we're concerned about is the price.

I'm of the opinion that unless it's to be closer to family and friends, any move ought to be the subject of great scrutiny by all parties involved. Even if it is a good idea, don't expect it to be easy. It sure wasn't for Angie.

I met her last year when she married the dad of one of my daughter's friends. He had been raising the little girl alone, so everyone was glad to see a woman on the scene. We were all busy with our own lives, so we didn't give her or where she came from a whole lot of thought. We heard that she was a teacher and had gotten a job at the middle school, but beyond that, a casual hello was as far as it went. After, I'm embarrassed to admit, a full year, I actually made the effort to get to know her. Turns out she married her husband after dating long distance for about ten months. She had never been married before, so she went from being a carefree single gal in Chicago to a suburban Atlanta mommy in one fell swoop. As she describes it:

> "I knew it would be hard, but I had no idea it would be this hard. I was really close to my dad and we saw each other at least once a week. I had a best friend I did everything with and I was a team leader at my school. I knew I would really miss those things, but I didn't realize I was going to miss everything else too. It was all those little daily things that made it the worst. One week I know everybody in town, the best place to get coffee, and all the great weekend hangouts. The next week, I can't find my way to the grocery store and I'm quickly realizing that parents don't spend a lot of time just hanging out on the weekends.
>
> I thought I'd feel more at home once school started, but with all the kids calling me by a name I can't even remember to answer to, I didn't feel like I knew anyone. Halfway through the year a single teacher joined our school and all the other single teachers immediately began asking her to do things with them. I guess they all assumed because I had a family I wouldn't be

interested. The married teachers were all into their own families, so I ended up not being part of either group. I came home every day in tears.

It took a long time, but I'm finally settling in. I've made some friends on the staff and in my neighborhood. I'm still happy I did it. I found a great guy and got a wonderful kid as part of the bargain. But I'm sure glad this first year is over."

.... ⚡ ....

FLASH
You might not need the connection, but maybe somebody else does.

....

You want to make a difference in somebody else's life? Try approaching the new girl. I don't know whether she's a co-worker, neighbor, or car pool mom. Just because we're so jaded by new people coming and going, doesn't mean they need any less support.

I have to wonder if the mommy crew didn't leap to embrace Angie because she's just a tad younger and more attractive than the rest of us. Showing up at the spring carnival in short shorts probably didn't help her cause much either. But how could she have known our unspoken rule about always looking a mess at all functions where our children are present?

You want to lose the perfect thing? Well, belly up to the bar and quit being so judgmental. Nowhere is losing our precon-ceived ideas about how things *should* be more important than with someone new. Keep in mind, they don't know the rules yet. And greeting them with a set of rules in hand is a horrible way to start.

Remember JoAnn's recently connected neighborhood? Apparently that warm feeling didn't extend to newcomers. Shortly after the tornado, the house at the end of the street sold, and what seemed to be a very nice family moved in. But then, horror of horrors, one of the first things they did was put a tire swing in their front yard. This homey touch did not meet with great approval from neighbors. A tire swing? In the front yard? And on the corner no less, right where everyone enters the neighborhood. And to make matters worse they put an inexpensive wrought-iron table and chairs right next to it.

Well that was just it! You would have thought these neighbors were the editors of *Beautiful Nonfunctional Yard* magazine rather than a bunch of middle-class homeowners. They decided that rather than talk to the new neighbors, they would send them a letter. So instead of being greeted by neighbors welcoming them, this family received a letter stating that their swing and table were inappropriate for a front yard. Could they please remove them and quit reducing everyone's property values?

No one knows where the family came from, what their situation was and yet they jumped all over them for breaking their rules. None of the self-appointed beautification committee bothered to notice that the only tree they had was in the front yard. For all any of this crew knew the parents think it looks terrible themselves and they only put it up because they promised the kids they could take it when they moved. As far as the table and chairs go, maybe they had the thought that, heaven forbid, some neighbors might like to join them in their yard.

You have every right to your own opinion regarding dress codes or lawn objects. But if you expect everyone else to abide by it you're going to be one frustrated and lonely cookie. Reading people the riot act regarding your local customs doesn't exactly endear you. And whether you inform them via memo or a disapproving look, I think you'll find that it's actually quite counterproductive. Not only does it make the person feel horrible, but you have little likelihood of ever getting your *should* enforced. Case in point, the tire swing and table remain, but I doubt the family has had a relaxed moment enjoying them since.

A few experiences like that and it's no wonder we don't try to connect with other people. Remember that good karma you've been spreading around at Wal-Mart? See if there's a little left for your own backyard. The next time someone moves in or joins whatever group you're in, spend a little time getting to know them before you decide whether they'll fit in or not. If they have half a brain they'll figure out the way things work soon enough.

Because you've lost trying to maintain a perfect image, you don't have to take a casserole or wear your best outfit. My guess is Angie wouldn't have minded if someone had shown up in sweats with a few grubby toddlers in tow. All you have to do is walk up to the person and say, "I know it must be hard to be new, what can I do to make it easier for you?" Trust me, they won't ask you to organize their Tupperware, they'll probably just want to know where the closest dry cleaner is. Since this takes no advance planning and only five minutes of your time I suggest you do it sooner rather than later. It would be great if you could beat the *should committee*.

Which brings me to another point: If you are the new person, don't mistake one or two negative people for a representative sample. JoAnn says that they come forward first because they're like mosquitoes looking for new blood. They've already alienated everyone else, so they've got to find some fresh meat. The rest of us with lives may not show up as fast, but give us a little time, we're coming.

For the record, JoAnn didn't sign that letter, but it was a few weeks before she made it over there to provide a nicer hello. Once she got to talking with them it turns out they were, no surprise, very hurt by the table memo. But they were also very receptive to her tactful offer of some "leftover" plants to screen it. Who do you think connected and made a difference?

Make it easy on yourself and everybody else; taking the high road is a lot more enjoyable.

REBEL WITH A CAUSE

I think of a house of worship as the place where:

A. Everyone wears their best clothes.

B. I keep meaning to get to but can't seem to get myself up on time to make it.

C. I threaten the kids within an inch of their lives to stay on their best behavior for once.

D. I can be my real self among a group of nonjudgmental friends.

Most of us got some sort of religious education when we were growing up. Whether it was Hebrew school, a youth group, vacation Bible study, or even just an occasional Sunday, we were usually raised as a something. For a lot of us, that something didn't have as much staying power when nobody was around to enforce it. It's another item on our *should list* we haven't quite gotten to.

I've heard that churches, synagogues, temples, and the lot are experiencing a resurgence in membership lately. Religious leaders may claim it's because we're all in the midst of a moral crisis. Or maybe it's starting to dawn on us that we want our kids to get the same lessons we got. I have to think that another reason for this renewed popularity is that we're looking for some connections. We want to go to a place with a few live bodies that care whether we show up or not. If you feel disconnected in your neighborhood and community, a church or synagogue seems like an obvious place to look for something better. But I wouldn't count on finding connections too easily in your house of worship either. At least not on the first pass, anyway.

Most congregations today are so big that you have a better likelihood of getting to know your seatmate at a rock concert. You can show up, sing, pray, kneel, meditate, or whatever and never make eye contact with a single person. A pastor friend of mine, Mark, has noticed it too. He says some of his congregation is practicing "helloship" instead of fellowship. "They'll smile and nod, but a lot of them don't take the time to really know each other." That's the regulars; it's even worse if you're still trying it on for size.

You think it's hard to figure out the social mores in a new neighborhood? Try going to a new church. It's confusing enough to remember when you're supposed to stand, kneel, or pray, but you've also got to figure out what to wear, say, and do so you don't embarrass yourself. It's one thing to stick to the tenets of a particular faith, but I've noticed there are usually a lot of other rules as well.

Oh I know, it's supposed to be about your personal relationship with a divine being, but don't tell me there isn't a whole lot of the perfect thing going around at church. The sad part is, a lot of people are finding themselves disconnected in the one place they ought to be unconditionally reconnected.

My friend Mark told me about a situation he just faced in his congregation. It seems that some of the teenage girls had been showing up in what certain members felt was inappropriate attire for church. These members approached him and asked if he could put a stop to it. Maybe ministers aren't supposed to get mad, but Mark sure was:

"Here they are, teenage girls who have woken up on Sunday morning to come to church, and these people want to harass them about what they're wearing? Don't they realize how lucky we are they came at all. If I started in on that they'd never come back."

I guess I'm not the only one that finds a holier-than-thou attitude more than a little ironic in church.

FLASH

Faith is about acceptance, not rejection.

Remember those negative mosquitoes that swarm on the newcomers? Well, a lot of them like to hang around churches too and there's nothing like a good set of rules to keep them fired up. It's a shame when there's no Mark around to temper them.

Not everyone lets that crew get in their way. Some people can find their faith no matter what's going on. My friend Beth is like that.

Beth is bright and funny and was everyone's favorite neighbor during the two brief years she lived on my street. I would also guess that there are a least a hundred other women across America that say the exact same thing about wonderful Beth. As her husband climbed the corporate ladder, Beth has had to move her family every two years during her entire fourteen-year marriage. That's seven houses, seven schools, seven moving vans, and seven times she had to say good-bye and start all over again.

As she describes it,

> "Every time I go into a new place, it's the same thing all over again. The kids don't want to start a new school again, my husband is all stressed over his new job, and I'm the one that has to make it all work."

As Beth told me this, she was facing move number eight and it was more than she could bear. Without giving you the sordid details, there were problems, and it wasn't all the moves. Divorce had been discussed and Beth was contemplating letting her husband go on alone.

But Beth had two children, and like many women she eventually decided that she meant what she said when she vowed for better or worse. The day the real estate agent posted the sign in her front yard, I knew her mind was made up. They would go and they would go as a family.

Poor Beth, I thought, she's going to be alone, again. You know what she told me?

> "I'm going, but I'm not going alone. There's one thing I've taken with me on every move we've ever made and that's my faith. It's the only companion I have sometimes, but it's always there for

me and it's never let me down. It waits for me at the end of a
long day and I can always find it just when I need it most."

Beth might not have any trouble finding her faith, but the rest of us usually need an actual address to get us started. With people moving in and out of communities like they're shipyards, there ought to be at least one familiar berth. Everyone deserves a place to go where they'll take you, no matter how rough the waters get. My stepmother, Judy, has found ten of them over the years. She's circled the country herself a few times, and it was due to a lot worse than a transfer.

Prior to meeting and marrying my father a few years back, Judy had the delightful experience of being married to an alcoholic for thirty years. Rather than give up booze, this chap thought the answer to his problems was a fresh start every two or three years. Somehow this new beginning never seemed to include gainful employment on his part. Charles Ingalls may have had the good grace to take his plow with him, but not this guy. So in addition to having to pack up, move, and settle into a new place, Judy always had to look for a job the minute she got there.

Their California move was the last straw:

"We were living in Michigan and it was the first time in our mar-
riage I actually felt settled. He had never found work, but I was
close to my sisters and had a great job, so this was the best
things had ever been for me. One day he comes home from 'job

hunting' again and says he thinks we would be better off in California. He just knew he could find a job there because the economy was better. I was a nurse, so I could get work anywhere, he reminded me.

I really didn't want to go, any more than I had wanted to make our other moves, but what could I do? He kept saying things were going to get better. I think I knew even then that they probably wouldn't, but I wanted so much to believe it, I went along with his plans. I didn't want it just for my sake, but for our daughter. She deserved a happy family and I kept thinking that at every new place we would turn into one.

I got a few leads on nursing jobs fairly quickly and off we went. We went on ahead of our furniture to find a rental house. It was much more expensive than we thought so we ended up with a really small house. I lined up a job, and so here I was trying to make it all work, one more time.

My husband was supposed to be out looking for work the day the truck was bringing our stuff. Although he had assured me that he had 'several options lined up,' as usual nothing materialized. I was at the house, waiting on the movers when he walked in. He looks around the empty house, turns to me and says, 'I don't like it here. We shouldn't have come.'

I felt sick to my stomach. I'd spent most of our savings, money I'd made working at night, to get us out there and now not only has he not even looked for a job, but he has the nerve to tell me this was a bad idea. That was it! I believed in the sanctity of marriage, but this wasn't marriage, it was insanity. I knew I had to get out. I worked long enough to save enough money for more movers, took my daughter back to Michigan, and filed for divorce.

At first I didn't think I'd have the strength to go through with it. I had no money, I worked nights in the ER, and sometimes I was so tired, I didn't see how I could get through another day. It was the worst time of my entire life.

I'd spent the better part of my life trying to make a marriage work and I had failed. We were Catholic and nobody from my family had ever gotten divorced. I felt like there was a scarlet D on my chest. The guilt was enormous. Maybe I should have tried harder, maybe I should have left earlier, maybe I never should have married him to begin with. I kept thinking it was my fault. What kind of mother leaves her child's father?

The only constant through the whole thing was my church. I went every Sunday and I never prayed harder in my life. When I was at church a calm would come over me. There was something so familiar and wonderful about the mass, the songs, and the prayers. It was like I was home. It was in those moments at church that I knew we would be OK."

No matter what religion you choose, you deserve to feel like Judy does. As you know I'm the last one to tell you what you *should* do. But if you decide organized religion is a place you can find it, here's a few things to keep in mind.

First, don't let the negative mosquitoes dissuade you. Unless they're the ones up on the pulpit, chances are they aren't a representative sample. But be careful, they sometimes appoint themselves head greeter and spokesperson so make sure you look around a bit before you make your decision.

Try not to let your past experiences make you too jaded. If your memory of religion is a nun rapping you on the hand with a ruler or some slick-haired guy spewing fire and brimstone, I can tell you things have changed. There's no rule that says you can't switch brands, so some investigation might be in order.

The other thing you need to realize is that congregations are looking for you as much as you might be looking for them. Without even knowing where you live, I can tell you with complete confidence that there are a number of churches, synagogues, and temples in your area that would love to have you knock at their door. So don't feel embarrassed about just showing up. If you're a bit rusty or confused about the rules just ask. I can guarantee someone will be happy to explain them. I'm not trying to hook you up with some overzealous evangelist, but if you're a bit shy, this is one place you don't have to worry about it.

One church I went to asked newcomers to raise their hands so they could give them a fresh loaf of homemade bread. I realized the brilliance of this strategy as I walked around afterwards holding my bread for all to see. As a clearly identified prospect, I can assure you there was no shortage of people eager to say hello.

If you do find somewhere you'd like to start attending, it helps if you buddy up with the regulars as fast as you can. In the old days when churches were small, people noticed if you didn't show up. In my husband's little town the minister came by your house afterwards to make sure you weren't sick. But if you're watching most of the service via closed-circuit TV it's hard to feel like you'd be missed. If regular attendance is your objective, making a few friends who also attend might ensure that you make it.

My friend Barbara went so far as to arrange the transportation:

> "We knew we had to start going to church after we had our kids. We had put it off for a while, but one night we were discussing it with some of our friends who were thinking the same thing. We decided that the only way we'd get around to going was if we made each other. Starting that Sunday we took turns picking each other up. It was a lot harder to justify sleeping late when you knew you'd have to answer the door in your bathrobe and explain why you couldn't go to church this week."

You can have the best intentions in the world, but there's nothing like a little peer pressure to make sure you follow up on them.

One of the best ways to get to know people is to get yourself into a smaller group. The official service might include shaking hands with your neighbor, but the way to really get to know them is in a smaller setting. Whether it's a Bible study, divorce recovery group, or coffee klatch, a more personal setting will make meeting people easier.

If you're already part of something you're happy with, remember some people are still looking, so go easy. I know it's exciting to think you might get a new one for your committee or group, but if you overwhelm them on the first visit you can scare them away. You don't know why they're there, where they came from, or what they're looking for. You're better off if you let them tell you before you try to sign them up.

The other thing to consider when it comes to prospects is that it's highly improbable that they're your clone. It's amazing to me how many congregations preach tolerance but are only willing to apply it to one of their own. Your membership drive isn't going to be very successful if you limit yourself to the perfect people, so I suggest you get over this one pretty quick.

Phillip Yancey, a noted religious journalist, exemplified it best when he describes a friend's experience in working with the down-and-out:

"A prostitute came to him in wretched straits, homeless, her health failing, unable to buy food for her two-year-old daughter. As she confessed the appalling things she had resorted to to support her drug habit, he could barely hear the sordid details of her story. He sat in complete silence not knowing what to say. At last he asked if she ever thought of going to a church for help. 'I will never forget the look of pure astonishment that crossed

her face,' he said. 'Church!' she cried. 'Why would I ever go there? They'd just make me feel worse than I already do!' "

I'm no biblical scholar, but the way I've read it, Jesus was a long-haired rebel with hooker friends. Try keeping that in mind the next time someone new shows up in the back pew.

I don't know where you stand with regard to your faith. And I'm not about to suggest any preferences. I'll leave that to your pastor, parents, or Sunday morning TV. But if you're looking for somewhere to connect and make a difference, they've already got these things up and running, so it's a pretty easy place to get started.

NOBODY.COM

I always like it when:

A. I can spend long hours in my car because it gives me time to consider potential solutions to the rain forest problem.

B. My health insurance company's voice mail system keeps me on hold long enough to hear the entire *Grease* soundtrack.

C. I sit at my computer all day answering E-mails and never speak to a live person.

D. Somebody asks how I'm doing and actually waits for the answer.

Our surroundings may have physically isolated us, but our lifestyles are making it even worse. It seems to me that the innovation and technology that were supposed to improve our lives is actually having the opposite effect.

How many times have you called a company, run through three voice mail menus, had to punch in your account number on each one, then got put on hold while you waited for a live person only to have them come on fifteen minutes later and ask you for your account number? Every organization I know would rather refer me to their Web site than actually speak with me. Heaven forbid they tell me what I need to know, better to let me wade through mountains of information and figure it out for myself.

They may expect you to understand their information, but the rest of the world isn't going to any great pains to keep itself current on us. It absolutely drives me crazy when I have to provide the same information over and over again to the same people. I can't tell you how many times, despite providing my insurance card, I've had to fill out lengthy forms for the same healthcare provider. It's hard not to feel like an anonymous drone if everywhere you turn people are more interested in your Social Security number than your name. And these people work for you! Things can get even more disconnected when you work for them.

For starters, who decided that working miles away from where you live was a good idea? Something about the quiet suburban lifestyle as I recall from our subdivision brochure. Oh yeah, and it was a hell of a lot cheaper than those quaint little homes in town. If you're a regular commuter, you know how awful the daily trip can be.

Hours of drive time presents several connection problems. The first and most obvious is, you're spending long hours alone in your car completely unconnected with anyone except possibly your local traffic reporter. But it's not exactly downtime, what with the traffic and a cell phone glued to your ear the whole ride.

Even if you're not driving it yourself, being jammed on a bus, ferry, or train with a bunch of strangers isn't much of a bonding exercise either. Put an experience like that on either end of a stress-filled day and there's not much time or brainpower left over for anything more meaningful.

Besides just the physical time and energy commutes drain from our lives, there's another connection problem that's not so obvious. If your office is like mine was, most of your co-workers also live a short highway away, but **it's not the same highway!** The result is work friends never come to your home and no one at work ever meets anyone from the rest of your life. Talk about dividing your life into little compartments. Your work may be a wonderful place to be, but let me ask you this: How many people at work really know you? I might be overly suspicious, but I've noticed it's pretty easy to present a perfect front when no one ever sees your house and your family exists only in a 5×7 frame you got for Christmas.

Don't get me wrong, being open about your personal life at

work isn't always such a great idea. The last thing I want you to do is take up your boss's time with all the gory details of your latest romance gone bad or daycare nightmares. Even co-workers aren't safe confidants these days with companies doing peer feedback. It might not make a whole lot of sense to spill your guts at the office; but if you spend most of your time with a bunch of people who don't really know you, it's going to affect you.

.... ⚡ ....

FLASH

When you don't get enough practice connecting, you forget how.

....

You might want to connect, but if you work, I wouldn't count on having many opportunities to do it. I've spent the last fifteen years in and out of a lot of businesses and I can tell you, the bar has definitely been raised. I don't care if you're the receptionist or the CEO, you've probably got more work and less time to do it in than a few years back. Dolly, Jane, and Lilly may have worked *9 to 5* and had some big yucks on company time, but the rest of us are clocking in a few more hours these days. Who can find the time to hatch hilarious plans to kill off the boss when we're too busy squeezing doctors appointments and errands into our lunch hours? Multiple E-mails and pro-ductivity measures don't leave many holes in the schedule for bonding with our coworkers either.

But hey, it's not like we've all got a big pool of candidates to choose from. My own prestigious office is an upstairs bedroom piled high with papers. Overall, working at home can be preferable to some long commute, but the only people at my watercooler are my kids screaming that it's empty. There's not a whole lot of bonding going on with them either. *Perfect Woman Worker* magazine may show mom at the laptop with a babe on each knee, but the reality is you've got to farm them off somewhere if you're going to get anything done. It's pretty pathetic when "you've got mail" is the only voice you hear all day.

If you don't have a paying job, the good news is you're not missing the camaraderie you thought you were. But don't think this disturbing trend is going to pass you by completely. As any management guru will tell you, when the worker bees aren't happy, they're a lot stingier with the honey.

Do you think that people aren't giving you that personal touch because they're evil villians who live to make your life miserable? Guess what? They're just giving you what they're getting. They can't take your phone call because they're still on hold for their boss whose overseas conference call with her boss has been delayed again. So, what can we do to make things a little more connected?

For starters, if you're a worker bee you might want to look up every now and again. My guess is you've probably got a few peers in the same boat you are. The next time you see one, share a little bit of yourself and you might be surprised at what you get back. Whether you go to lunch or chat on the phone, when you and your coworkers really know each other, work can be a lot more fun. Just because it's not high on the company's agenda doesn't mean you can't make it part of yours. Besides, I suspect those cavewomen ran a pretty efficient harvest once they got to know each other.

If you don't work or you're forced into virtual office solitude, see if there isn't a way to work a little watercooler time into your day. There are a lot of us out there and chances are even if we're not free for lunch, we wouldn't mind a call or two. But make sure that technology's working for you not against you. E-mail may be a great, cheap way to keep up with your old college roommate, but try not to let it take the place of real conversation. Faster isn't always better.

Just because our jobs, computers, and neighborhoods have disconnected us doesn't mean we can't scare up a few connections elsewhere. My friend Jennie even found one at the health club. As she says:

> "I was new to the area and hadn't met a soul yet. I work out of my home office, so the only people I get to talk with are clients on the phone or the UPS man. But one of the few things I usually do for myself is go exercise. I had seen this woman at the gym and she looked about my age. After a few weeks of noticing her in the same class, I decided I was going to approach her.
>
> In the past I never would have done something like that, but she seemed nice and always appeared to be in a good mood. I

figured what have I got to lose? Worst case scenario she's going to think I'm a bit odd. One day after class I walked up to her and said 'Hi, I'm Jennie, I know we don't know each other but I've seen you here several times. You look like a nice, normal person, would you like to go get a cup of coffee one day after class?' We went out that very day and over the course of a few months became friends. It never would have happened if I hadn't mustered up the nerve to approach her."

Desperate times call for desperate measures. Our environments and lifestyles are working against us so we're going to have to take some initiative here. You know all those bodies, voices, and cars getting in your way out there? Well, it helps if you remember they belong to actual people. They're a little tougher to spot these days so try not to get so lost in your Day-Timer you miss them.

The "please hold, fill out this form, resubmit your request" folks out there getting you down? Don't take it so personally, they're just doing the best they can with what they've got. It's easy to forget the person on the other side of the phone or window has a life if nobody ever seems to care about yours. A few nice comments to remind them you do care goes a long way in making things better for everyone.

Above all, don't let our anonymous culture do a number on you. The next time you feel like a lemming about to go over the cliff with the rest of the pack, say a kind word to the rodents around you. Who knows, a few of you may even decide to head back in the other direction.

JUST THE FACTS, MA'AM

It has been scientifically proven that women notice details more than men, especially when it comes to people. This of course, is because we're supposed to notice the cave kids and how other women are handling the planting, feeding, and birthing details of their lives. Our peers are still widely available, we've just quit noticing them. Modern barriers to connecting have left us with nowhere to use our connection wiring except to sitcoms, advertisements, and romance novels. We look right through those average frumpy-looking women at the mall and compare ourselves to the silicone enhanced, airbrushed teenager in the Victoria's Secret billboard instead.

Who can notice real people when "Miss Victoria" is presenting herself so prominently? We've gotten so busy and disconnected, we let her and her kind start setting our standards. The men may be using their wiring by ogling her, but she's not helping us one iota. The more involved you are with the people around you, the less she'll bother you. So in case your life has gotten so busy and unconnected you failed to notice, consider these facts:

The average American woman wears a size 14

One in two marriages end in divorce

74 percent of mothers with school-age children work

3 percent of Fortune 500 top-officer jobs are held by women

60 percent of people say the only time they clean their house is before company comes

And this just out—the psychiatric industry estimates that 97 percent of families are "dysfunctional."

You really have to wonder about any standard that leaves out the majority of the population. And don't go kidding yourself thinking that it's a recent development. Everybody's always had troubles, from the cave to the Cleavers.

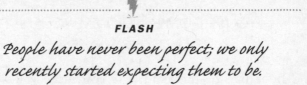

FLASH

*People have never been perfect; we only
recently started expecting them to be.*

The people around you are the normal ones. And the more exposure you have to them the better. So quit waiting for somebody better to come along. That 3 percent of functional people are spread way too thin to be bothered with the rest of us. If you're trying to connect, stick with the other 97 percent. We're not perfect, but then again neither are you.

CHAPTER FIVE

Last on the List

"I get by with a little help from my friends"

—*The Beatles*

YOU'RE GONNA NEED 'EM, YOU JUST DON'T KNOW WHEN

I hope that by this point I've convinced you how much friends can add to your life. Some of you might still think you're just too busy, so you've forced me to resort to desperate measures.

All the planning and hard work in the world doesn't spare us from these simple facts: Life isn't fair and bad stuff happens. At some point in time something is going to hit you—marital problems, a career crisis, sickness, children trouble, infertility, financial problems, or whatever. And to make matters worse it will probably have *something* to do with your family because it usually does. None of us get off scot-free.

That's why we need to have people beyond those who are "in" our daily lives. If you don't have someone who's not part of whatever trauma is going on to be there for you, you'll be alone. I know because that's what happened to my mother.

You may have noticed that I mentioned my mother's three children sitting in the front row at her funeral and that I also said I was the eldest of four. One of us wasn't at Mom's funeral, because thirteen years earlier we all sat in those same seats at his.

When my mother was forty years old, she lost her six-year-old son to meningitis. I'll spare you all the details, except to say it happened fast. One day he said he didn't feel good, the next day he was dead. And my mother had to live with it alone.

Why was this woman, who had done so much for everyone else, alone when her beloved child died? Because it's the worst part about this whole perfect nonsense; your fake self and the *should list* prevent you from having any real friends at all. My mother was an inspiring teacher, community activist, hard-working mother, and all those other things people said about her at her funeral. But she was so busy being all those things, that she never took the time to need a friend.

She could *be* a friend, but she was the kind of friend a lot of us "perfect strivers" are guilty of being and that's half a friend. The kind of friend who can be there for the other person, without letting others be there for you. Before my brother died, people didn't ever see my mother depressed or down. No one had seen her frustrated. No one saw her as anyone but someone to lean on. She never needed any help herself. She never gave anyone the gift of letting them *be* a friend to her. If people didn't feel close to her before, they certainly weren't going to jump in at the most awful moment of her life. I'm sorry to say that although a lot of people admired her, not many of them were really close to her.

Don't get me wrong, tons of people came to his funeral, there were lots of cards and flowers and the obligatory casseroles came. But no one was really there. No one felt like they knew her well enough to come over and drag her out of bed a month later when she needed it. No one knew her well enough to say, "Bullshit, tell me how you're really doing," when she said she was fine. No one knew how to just be with her.

FLASH

You better get the friends in place before you need them.

I said at the beginning of this book that a friend would have meant a world of difference to my mother. Not just when my brother died, but long before. When she was having the marital troubles typical of any long-standing marriage. Did she know everyone went through times like that? How could she? She handled it alone. The financial difficulties of raising four children? Once again, she soldiered on. Problems with a certain fifteen-year-old, who thought that the best use of her sopho- more year was to skip it and hang out with her nineteen-year- old, college-dropout boyfriend. I'm sure she was too em-

barrassed to ask for help or simply talk with someone about
what she was going through.

A few good friends can make a difference. I said that my
mother would have been surprised by her own funeral service
because I'm sure that she never knew how much she meant to
people. That's the other place those friends could have come
in. A friend would have pointed it out. A really good friend
would have made her look up from her *should list* and shown
my mother how much she mattered.

Rather than leave you in a puddle of tears over my mother's
missed opportunities, let's make sure *you* have some of those
real friends right now. You shouldn't have to wait for your
funeral, and I sure as hell don't want you going through some
awful time alone. I've given you a few places to get started, so
just pick one. You can look next door, at work, or make a friend
at the health club, but let's see if we can't find a way to ratchet
a few of those connections up a notch or two. The odds are
stacked against you out in the big, bad world, a few more players
on your side will even things up.

ALL YOUR EGGS IN ONE BASKET

I chose my friends because:

A. Our similar ideologies result in long, meaningful conversations about world events.

B. They were all willing to make the time and emotional commitment it takes to maintain a great friendship.

C. I searched high and low to create a diverse mix of people that would give me exposure to as many different lifestyles as possible.

D. They were there.

Former First Lady Betty Ford, says of the program at the Betty Ford Center, "a woman will do better in therapy if her group is all female. In a group that is coed, we have found, she tends to remain in the nurturing role, she hangs back. In an all-women group, she's not allowed to sit back. Another woman will say to her, What about *you*? How is this affecting *you*? How do *you* feel?"

Mrs. Ford would know. As a recovering alcoholic herself, she learned firsthand what the support of her women's group meant. As she says in her book, *Betty, a Glad Awakening,* "I will forever be grateful to them; they drove an hour here and an hour back, just to meet with me once a week." And as a woman, Mrs. Ford also knows what it's like to feel like you're responsible for everything and everyone. "My mother's voice was always in my ear, 'If you can't do it right, don't do it at all. . . . ' There are a lot of women like me who have done the church things and the book fairs and fixed meals and supervised homework— dedicated their days to someone else."

Women being women, most of us spend a lot of our time

in giving relationships. But you shouldn't have to be responsible for both sides of the happiness coin in *every* relationship you're in. Think about it, shrinks have shrinks and even priests still go to confession. They know you can't take on everyone else's troubles without an outlet for your own.

FLASH

You deserve to be the supportee sometimes.

It's pretty easy to forget you need support too when all *your* supportees are so vocal in their requests. Most of our friends are so busy with their own lists of things to do they're hardly clamoring for our attention. Given the demands on our time and bodies these days, the last thing we're going to make time for is each other. Maybe you aren't worried about this issue because it seems like you've already got a lot of friends.

Remember JoAnn's big vice president of marketing job? Well, as with most big jobs it kept her pretty busy. She didn't have time for a whole lot of outside interests beyond her family. It didn't bother her too much because she was so connected at work. She does a great job and is fun to be around, so naturally everyone really liked her. There were always people to go out to dinner with whenever she traveled and it always seemed like she had plenty of friends.

But one thing those big jobs tend to have in common is their fairly vulnerable status. As anyone who's been in corporate

America will tell you, the more visible you are, the more at risk you are. Especially when someone new comes in. For whatever reason, it seems like every time a new grand pooh-bah comes into any organization one of the first things they do is get rid of the second-in-command pooh-bah, who apparently have no value whatsoever because they worked for the previous poo-bah.

That's exactly what happened to JoAnn. She gave body and soul for over a dozen years, only to find out it was worth about six months severance.

> *"It wasn't a complete shock. They had already let a few other people go and I thought I might be next. Frankly I'm surprised I lasted as long as I did. It was still a blow though. They called it a reorganization, but it still felt like I was being fired.*
>
> *The worst part of it all was that on the way home I realized there wasn't anybody I could call. All the people I knew still worked there. The last thing they were going to do was risk their own jobs by aligning themselves with me."*

That's precisely why it's a good idea to have friends in more than one place. If something goes wrong it's nice to have somewhere else to turn. If you work, it's only natural that you would find a lot of your friends there. You obviously have something in common and they're certainly accessible. But remember, circumstances change and you're not going to spend your whole life in that job. Just because you spend a lot of time in a situation doesn't mean you have to limit your friendships to it.

What if all your friends are other couples and you suddenly find yourself having marital troubles? Wouldn't you like to have some friends that aren't friends with you both to talk about it with? Or what if it gets worse and you find yourself uncoupled? A divorce is bad enough without having to lose custody of all your friends in the bargain. Maybe you don't alter your marital status, you just change locations. I myself have been hugely disappointed at how quickly some friendships died after one us moved.

FLASH

A real friendship outlasts the situation that started it.

You may find your friends because circumstances put you together; but a real friendship isn't dependent on a place or situation to keep it alive. That's the difference between a friendship and an acquaintance. When friendships aren't dependent on situations we can play those supporter/supportee roles as the need arises.

In fact, sometimes I think our friends might be the only ones that truly have our best interests at heart, because they're the only ones whose lives won't be affected by our decisions. Even your own parents can't look at your life objectively. You don't believe me? Suppose you have just finished putting your child through college and medical school, and supplemented their income during the lean years of the internships and residency. Upon completion of this endeavor your offspring informs you that they may have made a mistake. Their true passion is poetry and perhaps they should have pursued that instead.

Only a friend can listen to this scenario and remain calm, because their egos aren't wrapped up in the situation. They're interested in you, your thoughts, and your feelings. They can hear you out without imposing their own agenda on the issue, and you don't usually have a lot of other agendas with them either.

Every woman I know has a running to-do list in her head. Sometimes our friends are the only people the list doesn't apply to. You may be a calm, serene soul who doesn't fret a moment when you're with your family, but I'm not five minutes into my designated quality time with my kids when I start looking around the house thinking what a mess things are. I have actually been out on a date with my husband where we spent the better part of the evening deciding whether or not we were going to refinance our house. You'd never waste an evening with a friend discussing such boring logistics. Your financial woes maybe, but I suspect the conversation with a friend would be more about the effect it's having on *you*, rather than the detailed plan to shore them up.

Remember, a real friendship works both ways. If you want someone to listen to your trouble talk you've got to be prepared to listen to their's. That means taking their world as seriously as you expect everyone to take yours. If you ask a friend, "How are you?" you've got to consider it an actual question, not just a pleasantry, because the answer isn't always going to be, "Just fine."

Not that mutual moaning is the only thing friends are good for. Some of the best fun I've ever had has been with my friends. It probably has something to do with the fact that they can pack for themselves and arrange their own transportation. Don't get me wrong, I love doing stuff with my family, but you have to admit it's a little more relaxing when you don't have to worry about whether the other person ate enough green stuff or how you're ever going to get them down for a nap. And I don't have a single friend that thinks wordlessly watching a ball game is a great way to spend the day together.

So if friends can add so much to our lives, why don't we make them a higher priority? I think one of the reasons is that our lives haven't been connected enough to find any. Friendships emerge from our existing connections; they're like the cream that rises. I'm no dairy farmer, but I doubt you're going to find a lot of cream if you never have any milk. Lots of connections keep you from coming up dry.

Beyond locating friends, I would have to say the biggest problem is the time it takes to hang on to them. When I was younger I used to spend long afternoons with my friends contemplating the nuances of every situation we'd encountered since we last talked. These days it's pretty hard to justify even a phone call when your checkbook hasn't been balanced in months and your family's down to the socks that don't match.

Most of us don't have the drawing power of a former first lady, so I doubt they're going to come to us. And the Psychic Friends Network is just way too expensive.

If you don't have a family and you're having trouble making the time, I have to wonder what you're doing with yourself. If you're letting a job fill all your hours, I'm going to play doctor and tell you the human body can only work so many hours before it rebels. Besides, even if you could maintain the pace, do you really want to? Establishing those kind of benchmarks is going to make it pretty tough if you ever decide to ratchet it back a notch or two. Next time you're tempted to crank out one more project or memo or whatever, think about JoAnn's ride home the day she got let go.

If you've put off your friends because of family demands, well, honey, I've walked a mile in your shoes and I'm here to tell you you're starting down a dangerous, lonely path. I know how it happens, but it's pretty pathetic when you find yourself all excited about the upcoming kid's birthday party at Circus World Pizza because you know you'll get to talk to some other moms. Sure it's better than having to work in the back making the pizza, but don't you deserve a few friends and events of your own choosing? Frankly, I think we all deserve a regular ladies' night out or at least an occasional lunch. I happen to think it does a family good to see that Mom has a life of her own.

If I can't talk you into anything that fun, I'm hoping you'll do something. My pals and I have resorted to some pretty low-brow rendezvous to keep a friendship alive.

We've been known to meet at fast-food joints and chat while we turn the kids loose in the ball pit. There's no cover charge and they never check to see if you bought their food. A few of us have even tried running our lunchtime errands together. Trust me, we all have the same lists and the line gives you at least five minutes talk time.

Don't want to fight the crowds? Save up all your catalogues, rent a video for the kids, and spend an evening doing your back-to-school shopping together. Sure your kids all end up with the same wardrobes, but at least they are not the only ones dressed in the discontinued sale stuff.

One friend of mine is so pushed for time that late at night, after she puts her kids to bed and her husband is vegged out in front of the tube, she meets her best friend at the twenty-four-hour grocery store. They have coffee in the snack bar, and catch up on each other's lives while they shop. It's not lunch at the Ritz, but hey, beggars can't be choosers. It beats spending an hour explaining why your children can't have any of the merchandise displayed in their hip-to-eye-level range.

A few of us have even been so desperate to connect we've been forced into utilizing technology. I'm not a big fan, but cell phones, pagers, faxes, and the like are productivity tools. I consider saving your sanity an appropriate use of these gadgets.

Just because you can't keep connected to your friends the way you used to, or even the way you'd like to, doesn't mean you can't do it at all. Take a lesson from Betty; even first ladies don't go it alone.

MADAME CHAIRPERSON

Whenever I'm faced with a difficult decision or problem I:

A. Get together my always-available friends and conduct a group brainstorming session, complete with flip charts and overheads.

B. Hope someone will really force me to do some "outside the box" thinking rather than just agreeing with my assessment.

C. Assign a numerical value to each component of the situation so that I can graph out the mean, median, and statistical variance.

D. Call up my best friend or my mother and whine about how tough my life is.

The other day my daughter came home from school all upset about who sat by who during lunch. It would appear that the second grade social caste system was not working in her favor and her life was a complete misery because of it. I may have let my own social life slip through the cracks, but like all the other self-sacrificing mommies out there, I wasn't about to let hers go down the tubes.

For once, I decided to take my own advice and discuss it with a friend before I took action. My friend Paula has a sensitive little soul in her family too, so I was sure if I called her I would at least get some reassurance mine was normal. Plus she's really funny and it always cheers me up to talk with her.

I got her on the phone and just as I was about to launch into the whole story she proceeds to tell me that she and her husband had gotten into a huge fight the night before, he had moved out, and they were divorcing. It wasn't a complete shock because I knew they had been having problems, but neither she nor I would have ever dreamed it would go this far this fast. Talk about a reality check: My little precious princess wasn't at the center of the in crowd, but hers was facing life without her dad in the house.

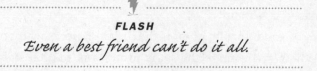

FLASH
Even a best friend can't do it all.

If you're lucky enough to have one, you know nobody could replace even her. But no matter how great, funny, smart, or multitalented they may be, they aren't always going to be available. Something is going to come up and they're going to be out of town, busy with their own personal crisis, or just plain uninterested in this particular topic.

Beyond support needs, I think there's another good reason to expand your circle a little bit. It's no coincidence that prisoners wear uniforms and are forced to eat, sleep, and walk the yard all on the same schedule. Or that whenever some movie wants to show a bleak vision of the future we're all dressed in identical, monochromatic outfits with the same expression on our faces. Being surrounded by a bunch of clones is boring and sometimes downright torture!

Everyone knows that any successful venture takes a group of diverse brains and talents to keep it going. Your life is no exception. King Arthur had his Round Table, presidents have their cabinets, and CEO's have their management teams. You deserve a committee of handpicked specialists assisting you as well.

Those other guys don't just choose their teams all willy-nilly and you don't have to either. If you've gotten yourself connected enough, you've got some options. Let's look at a typical friend collection:

A good starting point is the *in-the-trenches-with-you* friends. Whether you share the same profession, marital status, or geographic location, these are the people you can count on to listen to a my-life's-so-tough soliloquy and understand what you really mean. They'll also remind you when it's time to shut up and snap out of it. What's more, because their lives are pretty much the same as yours, they're also capable of telling you how important your role is whenever you need to hear it.

These type of friends are usually the easiest to make and keep because your lifestyles are so complementary. But only if you play it straight with them. You're going to have to listen to

their stuff as much as they do yours. Make it easy, let the good
and bad flow both ways; you'll save yourself a lot of set up time
if there's a crisis. Keep in mind, perfect queens are forced to
watch from the sidelines because they never get down *in the
trenches* with anybody. It's more fun to get down and dirty with
the rest of us.

Another type of friend that's been invaluable to me is the
wise woman. She's been there, done that, and can give you some
perspective on the subject. She's someone that's been through
whatever phase of life you're in right now. She didn't necessarily
handle everything perfectly, but she has to be willing to open
up about the gory details. I don't know about you but I'd much
rather learn from another person's regrets than have to experience my own.

You may have a sister, aunt, or mother to play this role for
you, but I've found an outsider doesn't get me quite as defensive
as my own family. Beyond some good advice, a *wise woman*
friend can remind you just how short this part of your life
actually is. Just knowing that JoAnn and her husband go off on
spur-of-the-moment trips and sleep late on the weekends gives
me hope for my future. And her honesty in admitting she wishes
she had some of those Chuck E. Cheese days back helps me
deal with the present.

On a purely logistical note, while these types of friends are
usually older, they don't have to be. If you're headed back into
work or marriage after a few decades off, your own daughter
might have a few words of insight on the topic.

You need wisdom, but you're also going to enjoy some wit, which brings me to the *wisecracking* friend. I hope all your friends have a good sense of humor, but even if you're the more serious type try to hook up with at least one of these. She may not be reliable, dependable, or remember your birthday, but at least you'll have someone to point out the lunacy of the world at large when you're so mired in it you can't see straight. I, of course, think this friend ranks at the top of the social pecking order.

As your years advance you're bound to find yourself with some younger or as I call them, *fresh friends*. These are the gals that remind you of just how far you've come. They're still struggling with all the issues and crises you either figured out or wisely abandoned years ago. While you might envy the perkiness of their bodies, I think you'll find they bring a fresh perspective to your life. I'm also convinced that maintaining a few younger friends will keep me from becoming old and stodgy before my time. If nothing else, you can count on them to call you on the carpet if you insist on wearing clothes and hairstyles a decade past their prime.

JoAnn says she likes being around younger people because it helps her relate to her son and his friends better. Another point on the *fresh friends,* remember how it's supposed to go both ways? Well the only way this *wise woman* thing is going to work is if somebody steps up to be one. Do your part and don't upset the balance of the universe.

Which brings me to another type of friend, the *good guy*.

And yes, by that I mean a male friend. The reality is you're going to have to live your life among them so you better get yourself a translator. Want to know why your husband or boss is acting like an insensitive stooge? The *good guy* can explain it to you. If you find a really *great guy* he'll be able to defend them *and* take your side all in the same conversation.

Unfortunately there aren't enough of these to go around, so a few of you are going to have to share. The only real criteria is that he's a man and he's willing to decode the mysteries of male behavior for you. Remember we're talking friends here, so don't go muddying the waters by thinking you can start having sex or raising children with him. Besides, if he's really a *good guy* he probably already has a mate of his own. This works out well, because you'll have to do some interpreting for him too. Throw in a few gift-giving suggestions and consider it your contribution to wives, employees, sisters, and mothers everywhere.

Go for some diversity with a few *not-my-life* friends. They can be married, single, mothers, or nuns. It doesn't matter. What you're looking for is someone to provide you with another perspective. It's easy to think yours is the only game in town if you never meet anyone that doesn't play in it.

These friends can remind you it's not all roses on their side of the fence either. I might be so mad at my husband I can't see straight, but one phone call from a single friend about her dating woes and he's lookin' a whole lot better. Now remember it's a friendship, not a competition. You're going to have to come clean with the gross stuff too. If you handle it right, you'll both be glad it's *not my life*.

Life may change, but everyone needs at least one *history friend*. Someone that's been an eyewitness to the ups, downs, and bad-hair decisions of your life. If you're lucky enough to have one of these, hang on for dear life. If you've lost touch, you might want to give her a call. Don't let geography or lifestyle changes come between you. Sure you've changed since you first hooked up with her, but I suspect there's a little bit of your old self left that would still enjoy talking with her.

Keep in mind, she remembers what you used to look like in a bathing suit and has the photos to prove it. She can burn them or have them made into posters. Stay close enough so she makes the right call.

So there you have it, your own personal dream team. I know I'm not allowed to add to your list unless I take something off, so remember the *should committee* from a few chapters back? Consider this their replacement. If this crew throws some advice your way, you might want to listen to it.

I HEARD IT THROUGH THE GRAPEVINE...

If I find out a bunch of my friends have been talking about me I:

A. Assume they must be very concerned about me to spend their valuable chat time on my affairs.

B. Guess I'm lucky that my life is so fascinating it can hold their interest.

C. Am really anxious to hear if any good advice came out of the session.

D. Feel completely betrayed.

I find it a lot easier to give advice than hear it. Much less take it. For example, I'm writing a book when I probably *should* be reading one. The truth is nobody likes to be told they're not doing it right. Especially if you didn't ask for an opinion in the first place.

There's so much advice out there though, sometimes it's hard to sift through it. Remember my friend Shannon, the former order barker who doesn't settle for "just fine" with her kids? Overachiever that she is, she takes being a mom pretty seriously and doesn't like to hear anybody telling her she's not up to par. But that's exactly what happened during her latest neighborhood playdate. While the kids were whooping it up, one of the other mothers saw fit to give her a string of unsolicited advice. She covered everything from her kids' diets to pet management. It sounds like the way I'd like to spend a sunny afternoon!

The second she got home Shannon called up her best friend Janine and recounted everything the woman said. While Janine joined her in righteous indignation on most of it, she was noticeably silent on a few points. In fact, when it came to the comments about her disorderly dogs Janine even said, "Well it's certainly something to think about."

FLASH

A real friend isn't always a "yes" friend.

Supporting you doesn't always mean agreeing with you. Some of the best advice I've ever gotten was when a true friend mustered up the courage and fortitude to tell me I was making a mess of things. A certain divorced friend reading me the riot act on how I better spend more time with my husband most immediately springs to mind.

Forget *Dear Abby* and *Cosmo* columns. If you've got the right friends in your life you've already got plenty of sources for great advice. The problem is most of us get so defensive at the hint of it, we fail to consider its merit. But once again, it's not all our fault. My experience has been that most people don't know how to deliver it. Any conversation that starts with, "Now I don't want to butt into your business but . . ." gets a rise out of me before I even know the topic.

Unfortunately the know-nothing busybodies are the first to speak up and the ones who actually have something to offer often keep their mouths shut. So how do we drill down to the good stuff? Well it helps if you start asking. You're already over being perfect, so this shouldn't be too big a leap. You know which friends give first-class advice because they're probably the ones that aren't too free with it. The next time you're faced with a problem instead of just moaning about it, check with your *committee* to see if they've got a few ideas on how to handle it.

Before you get all hysterical about how nobody understands the situation but you, let me say that I'm only asking you to listen to their advice. You're the one that gets to decide whether or not to take it. Besides, I suspect if you get to the point where you're asking for it, you probably already know what to do. You just want someone to confirm your decision.

There are going to be a few situations where some unsolicited intervention is appropriate though. That's another reason why you need a *committee*. Most of us have to hear something a few times to believe it—even if it is true. There's no way Shannon was going to give any credence to advice from a busybody neighbor but when her best friend agreed, it took on a little more credibility. Of course, she still had to get the rest of us to chime in before she was actually able to consider it viable.

Remember, your friends have your best interests at heart. Sometimes it's hard to hear, but if it's coming from more than one place you might want to think it over. If someone on the *committee* takes the time and trouble to tell you something, they've probably given it some thought before they brought it up. That's not to say they're always correct though.

My friend Paula is now paying spousal support to someone her *committee* actually approved of. She had taken a few wrong turns in the romance department before she met him and so she very wisely ran him by a few of her friends before making a long-term commitment. The verdict: He's a great guy, he's nice, and he's fun, he'll make a wonderful husband. Seven years, two kids, and a huge mortgage later it turns out the *committee* didn't think things through too well. Mr. Wonderful proved to be more than a little lacking when it came time to make the transition from fun hubby to responsible daddy.

Remember the *wise woman* and the *not-my-life* friends? It's helpful if a few of them are already at the place you're trying to get to. I firmly maintain that if Paula had had a few moms with little ones on the assignment we would have seen the danger signs. There's a big difference between a great hubby and a great daddy. You're talking two different job descriptions here. You're better off if you hire with the tougher job in mind. If you're not sure about the requirements, check with someone that knows from experience what's needed.

I also suggest you get comfortable with the *committee*'s ability to hold meetings without you. If you've culled a lot of your friends from one environment there's a high probability that they know each other. It's inevitable that at some point in time your name is going to come up in conversation. And not only your name, but some of your problems.

If you ever get wind of it, don't get all bent out of shape. Talking behind your back is when they start spreading rumors about your sex life. Analyzing your latest trials and tribulations means they care about you. You don't believe me? How often do people think or talk about their kids' lives when they aren't around? Doctors always discuss their toughest and most interesting cases with their colleagues. If you think you've been the subject of a friend caucus assume you're one of the interesting ones and be glad they think enough of you to bother.

Getting advice from a friend is one thing, giving it is another. Just because I think we can benefit from some of it, doesn't mean I'm suggesting you spread more of it around. In fact, I've found that the less you offer, the more effective it is. But that's a little bit easier said than done for some of us. How can we be expected to keep quiet when people so obviously need our help?

Buy yourself a muzzle if you have to. At the very least, wait a while before you jump in. They might figure it out for themselves or solicit an opinion in the meantime. Advice is always better received if they've asked for it. If they don't request it, you might want to take a minute before you volunteer your opinion to ask yourself, What's the worst-case scenario here? If it's not going to cost them a pile of time, tears, or money, is it really worth mentioning?

Another thing to consider, How sensitive is this topic? We all have our hot buttons so this will be different for everyone. For instance, you can say anything to me about my housekeeping, but I'm more touchy when it comes to my weight or wardrobe. One universal sore spot is our kids. Unless it's absolutely life threatening, stay away from this topic at all costs. There's not a woman alive that can hear negative feedback on her kids or her mothering without coming back at you with both barrels cocked. Suggest a book if you really think they need that much help.

Beyond the topic itself, think about what else is going on with the person. If they've already got a full plate, maybe your input on their problems or situation can wait for later. Nothing feels worse than having a friend sit in judgment of you when things are already going badly. Even good advice sounds like criticism when you're stressed to the max.

Having given you all the caveats, I will also tell you that a real friend doesn't let their friends screw up their lives without saying something. A real friend is willing to risk a fight to show how much she cares. If you've got a long track record of supporting each other, unsolicited advice won't ruin the friendship forever, it just may cool it for a while.

Whether requested by word or by deed, advice is still a bitter pill to swallow. Here's a few suggestions to make it go down easier:

The first is to look at it from their perspective. I've spent a lot of years in sales and I can tell you that the customer is more willing to listen to you if you've listened to them first. It doesn't matter if you've already analyzed this thing six ways to Sunday, they won't believe you get it until they tell you themselves. Show you understand their plan and situation before you unveil your solution.

Questions are a good way to get started. Instead of *telling* them how they *should* be handling something, ask them how they *are* handling it. Most people know when they have a problem, they just don't want other people pointing it out to them.

You'll be better off helping them figure out their own solution than trumpeting yours.

It's also a good idea to run your thoughts by somebody else before you try to bring it up. My husband's calm counsel has saved me from many "I'm going to tell her what I really think" speeches. Is it their need to hear it or your need to say it that's driving you? How would you feel if you were on the receiving end? Are you helping or just venting?

Putting yourself in their shoes helps you choose your words more carefully. Strong and to the point might work for a lawyer's closing argument, but you probably want to take a more subtle approach. Disclaimers like, "I may be way off base here," or, "I have a hard time with this too, but so and so suggested..." go a long way to soften the blow. Don't expect an immediate 180. You may have just passed on a life-changing gem, but it will probably take awhile to sink in.

Whether you're giving or receiving, think it through and keep their perspective in mind. Real friends know when to offer advice. Smart friends know when to take it.

WHO'S ZOOMIN' WHO?

The last time one of my friends said something really mean to me I:

A. Got completely defensive and starting accusing her of something even worse.

B. Wrote her off and never spoke to her again.

C. Cried for days because she had hurt my feelings.

D. Stayed calm and realized she was probably just having a bad day.

I've never been more hurt than when I felt like a friend turned on me. One minute you're soul mates and the next minute you're wondering why you ever connected in the first place. I'm usually so stressed-out all it takes is one insensitive comment to send me right over the edge. Fortunately everyone else I know isn't quite so thin-skinned. My friend Ann knows what it really means to be a friend.

She landed a big new account last year, but she couldn't do it all by herself. We're in the same business so she outsourced the fieldwork to me with the agreement that we would split the profits. It seemed like a fairly good project but as we got into it the client was difficult, the people complained all the time, and frankly I hated working with them. It was one of the most miserable assignments of my career. To make a long story short I started to feel like I was getting the short end of the stick. Here I was doing all this awful work with these obnoxious people and all she had to do was the front-end and back-office stuff. The last straw came when I had to run a training program for a group of heavy smokers in a room with no ventilation.

I called her up that night in a big huff saying I should keep more of the money because I was doing more than she was. She listened to me rant and rave for a few minutes and then she responded. A lesser friend would have pointed out that it was actually her client to begin with and I didn't have a leg to stand on. Or jumped all over my case for trying to renege on a good faith agreement. Or told me to take a hike and she would find somebody else. But she didn't do any of those things.

"It sounds like it was a really rough day and you aren't feeling too appreciated," she said. She was right, I wasn't mad at her, it was them. Fortunately, one of us had the brains and maturity to see it.

FLASH

Every action is not a reaction to you.

One of the things I've noticed about people, myself included, is that we have a hard time taking the other person's frame of mind into account. Anytime they act negative or the slightest bit pissy we assume it has something to do with us. Our first reaction is to think about the effect their behavior is having on us rather than why they might be doing it in the first place.

I hate to break it to you, but you are not the axis upon which the world rotates. Most of us begin to understand this concept after a few years of raising children, earning a living, or living with someone that still thinks they are. But it's hard to apply the same rules to our friends. After all, aren't these the people that aren't supposed to want anything from us?

Maybe they don't want anything from us, but maybe we can give it to them anyway. If you've ever flown off the handle at a kid, boss, client, employee, or husband, I doubt you got the same treatment Ann gave me. Women really are at the top of the food chain with regard to this particular skill. And the only way we're going to get that kind of support is if we give it to each other.

If one of your friends starts acting like a nut, take yourself out of the picture and try to figure out what's going on with her. Is she being terse and rude because she's so stressed-out she can't think straight? Maybe she hasn't returned your calls because her kids are sick and she's missed so much work she's staying up all night to catch up.

If you're really a pal like Ann, you'll even stay calm if she goes after you. Maybe she's jealous of whatever you have and she doesn't. Or maybe she's just had a bad day and you're the only person she feels safe unloading it on. I'm not asking you to play therapist here. And I certainly don't expect you to put up with a one-way friendship.

I am suggesting you cut your real friends some slack. Once again, it's not about accepting less, but having more. Once you realize everything they say isn't always directed at you, you'll spend a lot less time worrying about it. And you'll probably strengthen your friendship in the process.

Looking at it from their perspective doesn't just apply to the present either. I've known many a grown woman who is still smarting over some past ill inflicted years ago by someone that

was really doing the best they could at the time. If you're still
upset because your sister-in-law was such a sourpuss at your
wedding, it helps to remember she was only twenty at the time.

Besides their age and mind frame, if it happened a zillion
years ago, you really have to take the social context of the times
into account as well. Insight into personal relationships is a
fairly modern development. How many books like this were
available to your mother? The only advice mine got was from
Dr. Spock and *Ladies Home Journal*. Articles like, "Vegetables,
Frozen or Fresh?" weren't exactly consciousness raising.

If it happened a while ago, get over it and move on. They
probably didn't know any better and you're wasting valuable
brain space stewing over it. You can't rewrite the past, but you
can start making a difference in the future.

The next time one of your friends upsets you, think about
what's going on in their life before you take it personally. If
you're up to it, try to stay calm and ask. You might be the only
one that does. Remember, what comes around goes around and
once you demonstrate you're really on their side, I doubt they'll
ever forget it. Ann's got a few credits in her friend account, you
deserve some in yours.

PROUD MARY

Whenever someone tries to lend me a hand with something I:

**A. Feel totally embarrassed that they think I need so much
help.**

B. Can't believe she thinks I'm such a loser I need her to bail me out.

C. Wish I were one of those together people that could handle things on their own.

D. Graciously accept it.

There's an old Nigerian proverb that says, "Hold a true friend with both your hands." I think a lot of us only let our friends use one. We'll do something nice for someone else, but it's harder to let them do it for us. I know that whenever a friend does a favor for me, I'm never completely comfortable until I've returned it.

Jane was like that. She's an instructor at my health club and in my opinion she's one of the best. She uses everything from Broadway show tunes to country line-dancing to keep us in the room. As she says:

"It took me a long time to realize I didn't have to be some kick-butt instructor. I'm not some twenty-year-old with ripped abs, I'm a forty-year-old mother, who wants to lose ten pounds just like they do. These people have forced themselves to come, so the least I can do is make sure they have a good time. I know this is the only thing a lot of these women do for themselves all day. I want to make it fun, not intimidating."

Forget the hardbodies, we like Jane. And so does everybody else. She's active in her church, does PTA, and I am fully confident that if I moved in next door to her she would be at my door before the truck pulled away. She loves doing things for other people and I don't believe I've ever seen her without a smile on her face.

Not that she's an annoying *Perfect Queen*, mind you. She's fallen off the step in front of the whole class, her nails are a jaggedy mess, and she says ketchup counts as a vegetable in her house. The fact that she owns up to it and laughs about it is why we all like her so much.

But nobody was laughing when shortly before her thirty-ninth birthday Jane found out she had cancer. One of her breasts had been feeling strange for a while, so she went to the doctor to have it checked out. He didn't find a lump during the initial exam, but she insisted something was wrong; so he checked again and he found it. It was small, but it was also malignant. She knew her own body, she took charge, and so she caught it early enough for a good prognosis. But it was still cancer. She had to have a lumpectomy followed by several rounds of chemo and radiation.

Jane being Jane, it's no surprise that she had a lot of support. Everyone from her church, neighborhood, and health club wanted to be there for her. They showed up at the hospital, they brought food, offered to watch her kids and drive her to doctor's appointments. Her reaction:

"It was overwhelming, I couldn't believe I had that many friends. I would have never gotten through it without them. I felt like I had to be strong for my boys and most husbands just don't handle it well when the wife is sick. It was reassuring to know that other people were going to be strong for me. That emotional support really helped."

The offers for help around the house were another story though:

"I loved having people come see me, the cards, the letters, they meant a lot. But when they organized a plan for my family's meals, I felt like that was too much. I resisted a lot of the help because I felt guilty, they shouldn't have to cater to us.

But then I realized that maybe these people wanted to help for their benefit as much as mine. That other thinking, not wanting any help, that was all about me and what I had to prove.

It took a long time but I've come to understand—People want to help and thanking them makes them feel a lot better than refusing them."

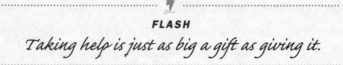

FLASH

Taking help is just as big a gift as giving it.

You know why most people say they can't or won't take help—pride. The way I see it, pride is a justifiable emotion when you've done something well. Turning down help from a friend isn't doing something well, it's doing something poorly. It's keeping them from holding on with both hands.

You like to know you make a difference to people. Don't you think your friends deserve the same thing? If we let ourselves get so wrapped up in trying to prove we're perfect, we'll never have the chance to let them. Every offer for help isn't an indication that they think you require it, it's just telling you they want to give it. A heartfelt thank-you leaves the giver feeling a lot better than disclaimers about how you don't really need it.

Some of us can't take a simple compliment. You know what I'm talking about. How many times have you sincerely complimented someone on something only to be told that you were incorrect? It wasn't that good, neat, pretty, organized, or whatever as you claimed. On the one hand we don't need any help, but on the other hand, heaven forbid someone telling us we're doing it well. Don't tell me I'm the only one that's ever worked her tail off on something and then claimed it was no big deal. Or spent hours making sure it was just right and then proceeded to point out the flaws to everyone who liked it.

On the face of it, this would seem like appropriate antiperfect queen behavior, but I think it's got its roots in the same place. Perfect people are supposed to be the givers not the receivers. Whether it's help or compliments, we're pretty reluctant to admit we need them. That little voice saying, "It's better to give than receive" has been drilled into us everywhere from our parents to vacation Bible school. True as that may be, it presents a bit of a logistical problem if we're all going in the same direction.

If a friend says or does something nice for you, think about *giving* them the kind of response you would like to hear. If they offer you some help, *give* them the gift of taking it. Graciously accept it and tell them how much it means to you. Be proud of the way you take it, not the way you refuse it. It doesn't mean you can't handle things, it means you don't have to.

You might think your friends are the last people you should take help from. After all, aren't they overloaded in their own lives already? Maybe. But I think when we complain about how much we're doing, what we're really upset about is that no one's bothered to notice. Take some help so you can be the one that does.

If you're the one offering, make it easy to accept. Vague offers of, "anything I can do" force the person to ask you to do something specific. It's like saying, "Tell me when you can't manage your life by yourself and I'll jump in." Things have to be pretty far gone for me to own up to that one. If you're a friend, you know them well enough to know what will help. Think about what might help you out if you were in the same situation. Just do whatever small or wonderful thing you think they'd like and make sure they know it was just as much for you as it was them.

I think one of the reasons we also have trouble taking compliments is because we don't get enough practice hearing them.

So you might want to throw a few of those toward your friends as well. But be careful here, insincere fawning doesn't cut it. And a favorable comparison to yourself doesn't count either. Comments like, "Oh, your house, body, kids, whatever are so great . . . especially when I compare them to mine," only result in them turning the comment back onto you. A real compliment is an accurate statement about how great *they're* doing.

If you're on the receiving end of a compliment, try considering the possibility that they might be right. Just because every piece of your life isn't perfect, doesn't mean you can't be proud of what's working well. You want to make someone's day better? Look them right in the eye, smile, and tell them they just made yours. People want to help other people to feel good about themselves, relax and let them.

Getting closer to our friends doesn't mean more work, it means less. Less of maintaining a perfect image and revealing more of the real you. Once you lose the pretense, you'll be able to make and keep some real friends. All they want from you is permission to do the same.

FLASH

Perfect doesn't last, friends do.

Finally, the way to get more friends is to be one. That means taking advice as well as giving it, listening as well as talking. And yes, even accepting some help or a compliment now and again. You'll know you're past perfect if all your friends can join in and admit it too. Hold on to each other with both hands. They deserve it and so do you.

CHAPTER SIX

What Did You Expect?

"I have learned from experience that the greater part of our happiness or misery depends on our dispositions and not on our circumstances."

—Martha Washington

WHICH END IS UP?

I don't know about you, but whenever I take on a new endeavor I always have a mental picture of how great it's going to be. It doesn't matter whether it's marriage, motherhood, or mashed potatoes. I'm always an optimist up front. It's the actual process that usually gets me down. Somehow it just never seems to go as smoothly as I've planned.

JoAnn's a lot like that too. Many years ago when she and her husband were both in graduate school they planned a canoeing and camping trip with several other students. JoAnn didn't have any experience, but she wasn't about to let that stand in her way. What she lacked in expertise she was going to make up for in preparation. She got a huge tent, every camping gadget available, and assembled all sorts of food she could prepare at the campsite. This was back in the days when people got their hair done once a week, so she rescheduled her appointment to the day before they left. Heavily loaded and freshly coiffed she was ready for some fun.

If you're an outdoor type you're probably already having a bit of a chuckle imagining JoAnn, new hairdo and all, trying to fit all the equipment and food into a narrow canoe. I guess when she heard "paddle down the river" she was picturing a scene out of *Tom Sawyer* where a big steam engine propels the mighty *Delta Queen* through the water.

Despite her initial disillusionment, they set off. JoAnn proved less than adept at the paddling, so her husband asked her to navigate. She had been told there were some rapids along the route and it was her job to look out for them. You can imagine her surprise when rapids turned out to be not just a place where the river went a little more rapidly, but several twisting, turning waterfalls in a row.

There was no way her husband could power through them without her help. Before they hit the first one he told her, "I'll steer, you just paddle backward when I tell you to." The canoe hit the rapids, pitching and turning, "Paddle backward, paddle backward," he shouted. JoAnn kept paddling, but the canoe kept going around in circles. He kept shouting, she kept paddling, and they eventually circled their way to the end. They were exhausted, all their gear was lost, and they were soaked to

the skin. The whole trip was a fiasco. The fact that they hadn't
capsized was a miracle.

They quickly abandoned the idea of going any farther, much less camping overnight with the rest of their group. They got out at the first available pickup point and took the bus back to their car. They headed for home, glowering at each other the whole way. JoAnn, who by now had a full-fledged migraine and was in desperate need of some aspirin, finally broke the silence by suggesting they stop. They found a gas station with a dingy coffee shop attached and as they sat down with their coffee, the inevitable fight ensued.

"I told you to paddle *backward*!" he shouted. "What did you think you were doing?"

"I was paddling backward!" she screamed. "Every time you bellowed at me, I put my paddle in and pulled it toward the back of the boat as hard as I could."

If you know anything about canoeing, you know that pulling your paddle toward the back of the boat is actually paddling forward. Now before you think JoAnn is totally clueless, let me remind you that this all happened twenty-five years ago. There were no outdoor shows on television, women didn't train for upper body strength, and the wilderness outfitting store didn't exist. She hadn't even been to 4-H camp, for heaven's sake. How was she supposed to know backward really meant forward and a ponytail was a more appropriate hairdo?

All she knew was that all their friends said it was going to be fun. She thought fun meant a mint julep and a chaise lounge.

When you start with the wrong picture,
you're never happy with the results.

JoAnn didn't know anything about canoeing so it wasn't her fault she dreamed up the wrong picture. Many of us are just as lacking in factual information when it comes to a lot of other endeavors as well. It's not like we start with a clean slate though. We've been force-fed the ideal image of everything from marriage to motherhood and from our work to our waistlines. We might not have the facts, but we're sure clear on the fantasy.

Stephen Covey has said, "Begin with the end in mind." Well I think a lot of us have gotten a little mixed up on which end we're going for here. Those perfect pictures are so deeply embedded in our heads, we assume they are the objective. But matching our lives to the picture isn't what makes them count.

Maybe things aren't going exactly the way you planned, but maybe it's not your fault, maybe you had the wrong end in mind. Take a minute to think about what you're really going for. Is it a life that runs smoothly every second of the day or the important stuff turning out OK in the end? Is it a beautifully presented dinner or a fun evening with friends? Is it a power career or a job you enjoy? Is it a marriage with no fighting or a partnership that lasts? Is it a home fit for a magazine or a place to hang out with your family? Is it wonderfully behaved children or adults that can make their way on their own?

The solution isn't always to just paddle harder. You don't want to wait until it's all over and you're sitting in some grungy gas station before you finally figure out the right direction. Let's look at a few of the "biggies" in our lives and think about the real objective. These situations might not all apply to you, at least not today. But be a sport and read them anyway. You never know when one of those *not my life* friends will need a boost.

CRY ME A RIVER

I can tell someone's really a great mother when:

A. She takes her brood to white tablecloth, four-star restaurants and the kids order in French.

B. Her children all hold hands wherever they go and have been known to offer each other the last piece of candy rather than fight over it.

C. She can wear all-silk clothing secure in the knowledge that spills and messes don't apply to her family.

D. She calls up her best friend every day screaming for moral support.

We might have that perfect picture in our heads when it comes to some aspects of our lives, but when it comes to motherhood, it's a Technicolor vision. That perfect person we all think is out there is probably a mother. Despite what may have happened during our own actual childhood and daily evidence to the contrary, her vision haunts us. She never shouts, she serves balanced meals on time, she's always calm, and nothing in her life ever goes wrong.

Every mother I know, myself included, measures herself against Perfect Mom and is forever coming up short. We're so stressed-out over this one, I could, and probably will, write a book on this one topic alone. When it comes to our kids, perfect doesn't even begin to describe the standards we hold ourselves to.

If you think the rest of the world perpetuates perfect in other areas, just try being a mother! We might be able to dismiss some of the advice on power dressing, but when it comes to our mothering, it's hard to ignore an entire industry devoted to helping you do it better. Not only are we determined to create the perfect childhood for our kids, but we're going to document it with photographs assembled creatively into albums as well.

Motherhood isn't for the fainthearted, as anyone who's done it knows. It might start off all pretty with baby showers and nursery decorating, but all that blood and pain during the delivery is the first clue it isn't going to be nonstop cute and cuddly. And if you became a mother by adoption, the pain, work, and not to mention money, it took to get you there, was a heads up for you as well.

Yet despite those early warning signs, a lot of us still cling to the notion that perfection exists and if we work hard enough we'll find it. I'm several years into the job myself and I'm still

convinced I can make everything just right. Although I just went
through a situation with my oldest daughter that was anything
but.

She had to wear a patch on one of her eyes to correct her
vision. If you've never worn one, I can tell you that it's miserable. It's basically a large Band-Aid worn over the good eye to
force the bad eye to work harder. In her case it's working, but
not very quickly. She was a good sport for the first few weeks,
but the novelty soon wore off and she started taking it off.
However, her doctor said we had a short period of time to
correct her vision and so she had to wear it for most of the day,
every day.

I tried all sorts of rewards at first, but when that didn't work
I became the patch police. I wrote notes to her teacher. Her
friends' parents were alerted that she must keep it on. I even
went so far as to start showing up at school during lunchtime.
As you can imagine this did not endear me to her.

We had a number of "let's figure out how we can handle
this together" talks, but I'm embarrassed to say, I also lost it a
few times. On one such occasion I believe my exact words were,
"Quit whining, it's for your own good, NOW DO IT!" shouted
three decibels above perfect mommy volume. This particular
round ended with a slammed door (hers) and a pillow full of
tears (mine). As I talked with JoAnn about it later in the week,
her comment was:

*"You know I had forgotten all about it until just now but I had to
wear an eye patch when I was in high school. Now that I think of*

it, I fought with my mother about it too. I guess there's no getting around it. It's going to be awful no matter how you handle it."

She was right. It was the pits. Here this poor kid is having to wear a patch on her eye for ten hours a day and I'm having to be the enforcer. There's no way this was going to be anything but miserable for both of us. The only thing making it worse was my heaping coals of fire on myself because my handling didn't turn it into a pleasurable experience.

All those magazines, shrinks, and radio show hosts have convinced us that perfect parenting is the cure for all our kids' ills. We've been given advice on how to cope with everything from sibling rivalry to divorce to peer pressure. And every bit of it implies that proper mommy management can make it OK.

Our kids are fighting again? We should have given them more quality time with Mom so they'd feel more secure. Our toddler wallops another kid at preschool? We should have taught them more appropriate outlets for their anger. Terrible manners in a restaurant? We should have given a lesson at home before we left. Can't get their chores done without constant nagging? We should have created a job chart complete with colorful stickers and stars. The kids overhear a parental screaming match? We should have demonstrated proper conflict resolution skills.

While some of this advice might be worthwhile, all these solutions make us feel like every time something doesn't go right, it's all our fault. Did anyone ever stop to consider that maybe it's just the nature of the beast? Kids have been whining, procrastinating, fighting, and choosing sweets over veggies since the dawn of time. The cave and Cleaver moms didn't think it was their fault because they didn't have the rest of the world chiming in on how to make it go away.

Beyond just those day-to-day nuisances, the other thing I've noticed is that we can't stand it when our kids are anything less than euphoric. And heaven forbid they're angry, uncomfortable, upset, or unhappy. If mom's really doing her job, that kind of stuff never happens. The fact that my precious princess had to experience the discomfort and embarrassment of an eye patch had me in absolute hysterics. After all, wasn't I supposed to protect her from things like this? Shouldn't I have caught it earlier? There had to be a way I could fix it without causing her so much anguish.

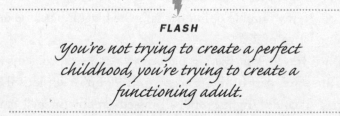

FLASH

You're not trying to create a perfect childhood, you're trying to create a functioning adult.

I don't know if you're trying to re-create the childhood you think you had, or the one you wish you had. But I'm guessing you're going for the childhood with no tears, shouting, messes, or fights. Every time these disruptions enter the picture, we consider it evidence that we're not up to the job.

But that stuff doesn't prove you're doing it wrong, it just proves you're doing it.

I know we all want to do the best for our kids, but you really have to think about your objectives. If every moment of their childhood goes perfectly, how are they going to feel when their adulthood doesn't measure up? Do you honestly think your child is going to waltz through life and never be shouted at, treated unfairly, or ignored? Or perhaps you're harboring the illusion that their life will never include hurt feelings, burnt meals, or hard work. Trust me, difficulties are a lot harder to handle if they take you by surprise.

You don't need to create disharmony or problems, they're going to happen whether you like it or not. But if you beat yourself up every time they do, you'll be black-and-blue before it's over. Nowhere is the perfect picture in your head more unrealistic and counterproductive than when it comes to motherhood. In my humble opinion, that's the biggest place we deserve to let go of it.

Once you look at the big picture you can see problems as what they are, part of the process. And if you've got kids that process includes fights, spills, missed appointments, and maybe even a few rounds of head lice along the way. You're not going for perfect, you're going for better. And better means realizing that preparing kids for adulthood doesn't mean guaranteeing their happiness twenty-four hours a day.

My personal theory is, if you've never had one of your kids scream, "I hate you, I hate you, I hate you" and then run crying into their room, you're not doing your job. You're either hopelessly permissive or your child is so repressed they'll probably die of an ulcer by the time they're thirty. My father puts it another way, "If your children never give you a bit of trouble, you are raising the most boring people alive." Well, my siblings and I must be wildly exciting.

If you're not feeling too great about the parenting job you're doing, take a look at your measurement tool. Are you going for the picture or are you preparing your kids for reality? Remember, the report cards and performance reviews on this one don't come until the end, when the trainees have to step into the job themselves. Once they do, they're usually a lot more forgiving of your methods.

Since thirty years is too long to wait for some meaningful feedback, I suggest you give yourself some now. Or better yet, you and some of your *in-the-trenches* friends can do it for each other. The next time you're overwhelmed, take a few minutes to remind each other that perfect childhoods don't result in perfect adults, they result in unprepared and disappointed ones.

If you're showing up for mothering, I can already tell you you're making a difference. There's nobody that loves your kids like you do and I'm sure there's nobody working harder to make sure they turn out right. If the messy house, fast-food meals, and occasional mental breakdowns are making you feel like you're not up for the job, keep in mind, your kids are going to be comparing themselves to you one day. Do you want to be the perfect image that haunts them or the one that gives them permission to cut themselves a little slack? I doubt Wally and the Beave's wives felt too comfortable sharing their parental mishaps with June. Do everybody a favor and keep the bar at a reasonable height.

Your kids might only get one chance at childhood, but hands-on motherhood is a pretty short gig too. Don't you think you deserve to enjoy it? Quit letting the pursuit of perfection ruin it for you. Just because it's loud, messy, and dirty doesn't mean it's going wrong. It usually means it's going right.

THE TROUBLE WITH WORK

The thing I like best about my work is:

A. The fact that I'm always able to get everything done exactly the way it should be and am never late on anything.

B. How everyone goes out of their way to make every experience as personal as possible.

C. The leisurely pace of it since it allows me plenty of time to chat with my friends.

D. When I'm done with it.

When it comes to work, women expect more than men do, at least in terms of emotional fulfillment. Most of the men I know grew up with the notion that work was going to be hard and since you had to do it anyway, you better just get used to it. Get good at it and you could make some real money and garner a little recognition along the way. Happiness was the result, not part of the process.

Women are different; we want our jobs to mean something to us and to everybody else. After all, weren't great careers something women like my mother didn't get to have? It's pretty hard not to have lofty expectations when the whole generation before you fought to pave your way. Well, you may be ecstatic about your job, but all the articles I see outlining the steps to an early retirement lead me to believe everyone else is not quite so enamored with theirs.

Talk to anyone about their work for any length of time and you'll find out there's something they don't like about it. Or rather someone. I don't know if it's the boss, the coworkers, the customers, or the subordinates, but I'm guessing somebody out there is keeping it from going the way it *should* be. Maybe they take it too seriously or maybe not seriously enough. They give too much direction or not enough. They work too slow or too fast. They talk too much or too little. Whether it's the fact that they're not committed enough or you think they should *be* committed, I'm betting you get more irritated with them than you do the work itself.

Men might have the same frustrations, but they don't seem to take it quite as personally as we do. They can barely remember what a coworker said over lunch, much less lie awake at night ruminating over it. But when you're wired to connect with people you just naturally process things from a personal perspective.

I was reading an interview with some famous coach who talked about the difference between coaching men and women. He said, "You can stand up in front of a men's team and give them a lecture on how everybody needs to work on strength training and the guys all look around thinking, 'I'm in great shape, but he's right, the rest of this crew really needs to tone up.' Say the same thing to a women's team and every player in the room will think you're talking specifically to her."

It's easy to lose your perspective if you only see things from your point of view. Keep in mind, everybody else doesn't have the same perfect picture in their brain that you do. And when it comes to work, your picture is usually a small piece of the bigger one. But women aren't the only ones that sometimes lose sight of that. My friend Steve works for a small, privately held training company and was pretty miffed at the way his boss, the president, was handling their expansion.

"She was really intent on making all these acquisitions. She would look for small firms that were willing to sell; their programs weren't nearly as important as what their P and L looked like. All she cared about was making the balance sheet look good so that she could take the company public next year.

Everybody was talking about how hard she was making things for us, when all of a sudden I realized . . . of course she's focused on the money, that's what the owner hired her for."

Work is set up to make money, not happiness.

Your job might make you happy sometimes, but I doubt your organization is set up with that in mind. The bottom line is companies exist to make a profit, either for an owner or the stockholders. Even if your organization has some great mission about how they benefit society, what got more pages in the annual report? Their philanthropic efforts or the financials?

Now before you get all disgusted with the pack of money-grubbers running your world, let me ask you this: Would you show up if you weren't paid? I don't mean to imply that work is only about the money. Work can be fun, exciting, creative, and a whole host of other great things, but we're setting ourselves up for disappointment if we expect it to be that all the time. This was a tough lesson for me to learn, but the quicker you're clear on the money issue, the easier time you'll have understanding why some things go the way they do.

You may work in the public sector serving the good of humanity, but don't go kidding yourself thinking somebody's not checking on your books too. Even if you work for free for some great nonprofit organization, the only way you're going to be able to keep doing it is if they have the money to run it.

I've heard that the workplace is becoming the new community. That might be true, but I find the thought a little disconcerting. After all, communities are usually based on people, not profits. They develop naturally as people connect with one another. The work environment doesn't just develop; it's set up with a definite agenda right from the start. Whether the goal is proceeds or productivity, the number one objective is to make sure they get them.

I think one of the ways we get ourselves in trouble over work is we fail to realize its true purpose. You know those people you're always so frustrated with on the job? They weren't brought into the organization because someone thought you'd all enjoy getting to know each other better. They were hired because somebody thought they had the skills to get the job done. It's about results. When people are getting them, most companies aren't even very picky about how they did it. And if you're a stockholder, I doubt you'd want it any other way.

Your organization may spend a lot of time and money putting you through team-building training, but don't make the mistake of thinking that's the end result. As someone that's run some of those training sessions, I can assure you, they're being done with the bottom line in mind. Some of the individual *people* in your organization may care very much about you, but the establishment itself exists for an entirely different reason. Get your mind around that and the rest of the stuff will be a lot easier to deal with.

When you know the organization's goals, you can't take everything personally. If someone asks for more work than you want to do, or wants you to do it in a different way than you'd

like to, don't assume they're trying to make your life miserable.
Maybe they're just trying to get their job done and asking for
more from you is the only way they know how. I don't know
if they're trying to get better results for themselves or if they're
just focused on the task at hand. Whatever it is, it probably has
more to do with *their* boss than it does you.

Maybe you are the boss and you're the one getting the pressure from upstairs. You know what needs to be done; the problem is the rest of this crew just doesn't get it. Before you jump
to the conclusion that it's a plot to make you look bad, take a
minute to consider what else they're doing. Do you really think
they're hell-bent on letting you down? Maybe they're just being
pulled in so many directions they can't see straight. Or perhaps
they're doing a lot of work, it's just not the right work. Without
turning this into a management class, you might want to check
and see if they know what you want. I doubt you hired The
Amazing Kreskin, so you can't expect them to read your mind.
Even if you do reach the conclusion that they're just flat-out
lazy, don't you think they acquired that trait before they went
to work for you? The important thing to remember here is their
job performance has more to do with them than it does you.

You're always going to have conflicts with the people you
work with, but if you can try not to take it personally you won't
find yourself stewing about them for so long. In fact, I've found
that once you realize most people are just trying to do their
jobs, you can move beyond some of those work logistics and
have a real relationship if you want to. You don't have to quit

liking them just because you had a difference of opinion. Keep in mind they didn't get the memo on your version of perfect, so you can't always expect them to adhere to it.

Which brings me to another problem a lot of us have with work. That perfect picture we're working toward includes some pretty high standards on our part as well. You know how the coach says every woman thinks she's the only one that doesn't measure up. Besides taking everything personally, I think we tend to focus more on what we didn't get done than what we did. For some reason it's impossible for us to feel like we did a good job if there's one thing left undone.

My friend Ann had to get comfortable with everything being less than perfect. Several years ago she was put in charge of her company's European division. The job was very demanding, but with a lot of hard work, she was able to pull it off. Just when she felt like she had things under control, her boss gave her a big new assignment. There was no way she could do it at the same time she managed everything else. Never one to whine, she proactively went back to her boss and very logically laid out all of her assignments and the time it would take to get them done correctly. Based on his top priorities what would he like her to do and what should she eliminate? His answer?

"Nothing. And I don't expect you to put in any more hours either. You don't have to get all this stuff done perfectly, just get it done good enough. You're so used to being a star student you think

you need to get an A on everything. Be willing to take a C on

some of the stuff that's not so important."

201

WHAT DID YOU EXPECT?

This guy is my dream boss. If you're having trouble getting it all done the way you'd like, ask yourself, what bad thing happens if this part isn't quite up to my standards? If the answer is nothing, move on. Once again it's about the results, not the process. You're going to feel better by making a real contribution, not getting tied up in the minutia.

But not everybody's got a boss like Ann's. Some of you may have the unpleasant experience of working for someone that believes perfect is the only way to do anything. In this situation it's really going to be up to you to get as much clarification on the priorities as you can. Isn't there at least one C item? If you work for a hopeless nitpicker, you more than anyone else, need to keep in mind the earlier advice about not taking it so personally. I don't know if they're on your case because they think they have to be or because they don't have anything else to do. Before you get hysterical, let me remind you, it's the boss's job to get more out of less. They don't get paid to tell you you're doing everything right, your mother can do that for free.

Sometimes it does have to be perfect every time. I know I wouldn't want a heart surgeon that got most of my operation right. And if I'm driving across a bridge I want every inch of it to be stable, not just 90 percent. If you've got a job like that, all I can tell you is try to differentiate between the work and the conditions. You might have to get your part just so, but it's pretty unrealistic to expect everything else around you to be the same. Make sure you're clear on the piece that really matters. As long as that bridge is safe, nobody cares if there were coffee stains on the plan.

Not taking things personally and focusing on the big picture makes work easier to tolerate, but what about that meaning we're looking for? Is there any way we can find it when everybody else is more concerned about making a buck and covering their hides? I think you can. And you don't have to look too hard either.

Making money and making a difference don't have to be in conflict. Once you *de*personalize all that other stuff, it frees you up to personalize your part. I don't know what you do, but I'm guessing doing it well affects somebody. It could be the customers, the management team, or just the other people that get to keep their jobs because you do yours. Corporations may only exist on paper, but the people you work with are very real indeed. Instead of wasting your time questioning their motives or mission, give them the benefit of the doubt and make dealing with you one of the good parts of their day.

Adding your personal touch doesn't mean you have to reinvent the wheel on every project. In fact, half the time you're better off if you don't even try. My father had a job where he had to choose vendors for a number of different projects. Despite the extensive guidelines they sent out for proposals, most of them came back with some unique twist. He was continually amazed. "We've told these people exactly what they need to do to get the business. Why can't they just do it?"

I don't want to stifle your creativity here, but don't make things harder than they have to be. If they put the directions on the box, just follow them. They're there for a reason. It doesn't always take some flash of brilliance or a complete 180 to make a difference at work. Sometimes it's as simple as taking the job you were assigned and making it meaningful to you and the people you interact with.

For some people it's pretty easy to see how their job connects with others. A few of you might have even chosen your profession with that thought in mind. My sister, a highly motivated, change-the-world GenXer, works in public health handling community communications. She says,

> *"The person that had my job before me didn't do anything more than just go through the motions. Didn't he get it? This job is about people's lives and making sure they're safe. I'm not going to put out a bunch of boring memos people will never read. I'm going to make sure I really do something for them."*

It's all in how you look at it. If you've got that kind of attitude about your work, I'm sure you do a great job and everybody around you knows it. The hardest part of a job like that is not getting too upset when you find out the rest of the world doesn't share your missionary zeal. Try to keep in mind, everybody's job isn't quite as interesting as yours and sometimes they've been doing it a lot longer. Some of us crazy nuts have another even harder job outside the office.

Juggling work and family is a balancing act I never feel like I've mastered. I know how hard it is, but just because you want to put your family first, doesn't mean you have to enjoy your work any less. In fact, I humbly suggest if you're going to have to leave your kids to do it, you deserve to enjoy it even more. There's no way I'm going to put on panty hose, hire a babysitter, get in my car, and drive somewhere if I don't think it matters to somebody. It would be a shame to let the guilt of what you've left behind keep you from seeing how your job matters.

If I haven't helped to make your paid job feel more meaningful to you, I can tell you your paycheck sure is. Just because your husband's got a decent job, doesn't mean you're some materialistic shrew if you have one too. Unless you're blowing it on lottery tickets or things you and your family don't need, the money you make matters to your family. Men think of earning a living as something they do *for* their families, not *against* their families. Single mothers are real clear on this concept. Married ones can be too.

No matter what your personal circumstances are, you deserve to know your work matters to someone. You're going to spend the better part of the day on it, so focus on the parts that count and it will be a lot more enjoyable. You don't have to change the world, you can just change your part in it.

When I was a little girl I dreamed that one day I would meet a man who would:

A. Sweep me off my feet with his dashing good looks and charm.

B. Pen me love letters destined to become romantic classics recited by generations of lovers to come.

C. Share his innermost thoughts and emotions with me.

D. Show up when I really need him.

If you're in any kind of long-term relationship, you're probably already over perfect. Let's be honest here, there's no way you can share a checkbook, television, and bathroom with someone and not encounter a few problems. Pair up with Mother Teresa and you might keep the squabbling to a minimum, but anyone that's cohabitated with a man will tell you, it's no picnic. Throw the stress of a few kids into the mix and it's a wonder any of us survive.

Most of the women I know let go of the perfect picture pretty early in the game on this one. It's not that we don't crave that romantic soul mate connection with every fiber of our being. But when the other side refuses to read, much less discuss the latest *Cosmo* couples quiz, it's pretty obvious we're going to have to get over it. At least this time we don't have to beat ourselves up about it. I mean, we know what it *should* look like, it's not our fault he won't play along.

If you're like me, you probably went into marriage convinced you were going to have a better relationship than the one your parents had. Whether you were going to play a new role or he was, it was somehow going to be different. Right? Not as many fights, more time together, more communication, and certainly a lot more romance. Oh, and he was going to be a much more willing participant in all that stuff around the house too. Well guess what? You may have gotten yourself a newer model, but you probably still got him from the same dealership. Even if you drove home a spiffier one, I doubt the garage you parked him in was as different as you hoped it would be.

Just like a lot of our other big endeavors, nobody bothered to fill us in on this one either. That is unless you call witnessing an actual relationship some sort of reality check. Despite all this talk about modern partnerships, a lot of the elements of relationships remain the same as they always were. There's still the laundry, the dishes, the bills, and all the other stuff that goes along with sharing a life together. It's doesn't matter who you're doing it with or what decade you're doing it in, it's hard. But just try telling that to someone that hasn't done it yet.

I was planning a lunch date with my friend Susan and we thought that instead of meeting for our usual burger and fries we might actually go to a decent restaurant. As we tried to figure out a place, she said, "Well, you would know where to go better than I would. You're married, so you probably go out a lot more." Susan is not married and as you can tell from that comment she has obviously never been married. For some unfathomable reason, she believed that marriage involved a lot of movies, restaurants, and good times. I guess she'd dated over the years and so she assumed marriage was just more of the same. Either that or she's been taking some of her reading a little too seriously.

I was at the hairdresser the other day and since one of my *fresh friends* has me going to a hipper place, they didn't have the usual *Matronly Mom* magazines available. The only things to read were big, fat glossies with skinny models on the cover. So instead of reading about which outfits best cover a tummy bulge, I learned all about "entrances that make heads turn" and "third-date dialogue." I couldn't believe how many subtle nuances there were to dating. Everything from lip liner that lasts until morning to minding your p's and q's at a baseball game with his buddies. Every single article was to help you snag and keep the perfect guy. The amazing thing was, these articles actually implied that the advice was somehow relevant to a long-term relationship.

In the spirit of full disclosure, I have to tell you that I've been married for fifteen years and the last time I dated, a guy that could afford to pay for your beer and stayed sober enough to drive you home constituted a dream man. But it seems to me like all this information out there about men might be leading a few of you down the wrong path. Once you've read "What Mr. Shy Guy Really Wants You to Know," how is "Mr. Work All Day" who falls asleep on the couch ever going to measure up?

.... ⚡ ....

FLASH

Dating is about fun, marriage is about work.

....

You'd think it would be pretty obvious. I mean just look at the difference in the activities. Dating means dinners, fancy home tours, and movies; talking about those fun activities and then actually doing them. Marriage means making the dinners, cleaning your own home, and taking the kids to the movies. Oh sure, you still talk about what your weekend plans are, but a conversation about who's going to get the house picked up for the in-law visit isn't nearly as fun as deciding which restaurant to go to.

Lip liner may help you find a man, living with one takes a little more effort. But not to worry. There's a plethora of offerings on that too. Heaven knows, with all the books, tapes, seminars, and counselors available, we've got all the tools we need to create the perfect partnership. Everybody's got the recipe for producing a match made in heaven. It must exist, the brochure for the couple's communication retreat promised it!

Anybody with half a brain knows that any kind of long-term relationship is going to take some work, but I'm sick of everybody implying that there's a shared-responsibility, multiple orgasm, talk-it-all-through couple out there. And, that after a few more books and counseling sessions we can become part of one. I've read and heard the same stuff you have and it makes me tired just to think about it.

Besides, being my cynical self here, I've checked out the background on a few of the experts. Guess what? The 50 percent divorce rate applies to them too. I've known a few of those touchy-feely counselor types in my day and you might be surprised at what a mess some of their personal lives are. Excellent interpersonal skills can only take a couple so far.

I have to wonder that, maybe more work *on* the relationship isn't the only the answer. How about less work *during* it? Instead of working so hard pursuing the perfect partnership, maybe we ought to schedule a little time to enjoy the one we've got. If you're less than delighted with your current arrangement, ask yourself: Is it really the players? Or is it the conditions you're doing it in?

My father has experienced what a difference a change of circumstances can make. A few years after my mother's death he married Judy, a wonderful woman who, like him, had completed a lifetime of parenting and hard work and was now ready for some fun. His comment on the situation: "You know, when you don't have jobs, kids, or bills to worry about, this whole marriage thing is a lot easier." Well *hello*, of course it's more fun—they're retired, they live on a lake, and all their in-laws are dead. Sounds like one big, long date to me.

If you're in one of those types of relationships, all I ask is that you remind the rest of us that they exist somewhere out there on the future horizon. If you're in the other type, the kind that includes work, children, house payments, and a phone that never quits ringing, let's see what can be done to perk up the present for you. Like I said, since you're over perfect, go for better. That lake house is a lot more fun if you're still on speaking terms when you get there.

When you're in it for the long haul, a firm grip on reality is a must. If you're still looking or considering trading your spouse in, you might want to pay attention. When it comes to unmet expectations, there seem to be a few universal ones. Once you realize they're part of the standard equipment, maybe you won't be so quick to decide you got a lemon.

One biggie is communication. Whether it's quantity, quality, or both, there aren't too many men out there who can meet our requirements. A therapist friend of mine goes so far as to say, "the problem with most relationships is that women keep trying to get men to share their innermost thoughts and most men don't have any."

The bottom line is that you're probably wired for more connecting than he is so you're going to have to look somewhere else to pick up the slack. Remember those *in-the-trenches* friends? The more connecting you do with them, the less frustrated you'll be when he falls asleep during your dissertation on the meaning of life. If your relationship meets 95 percent of his connection needs, but only 25 percent of yours, simple math-

ematics tells you there's going to be a problem. Save yourself a
fight and get the balance elsewhere.

Connecting isn't the only way friends can fill in the gaps. Just because your partner doesn't want to do something with you, doesn't mean you can't do it. I'm always amazed at how many women turn down invitations or don't do things they really like just because the husband doesn't want to go. Worse than just missing out, you'll resent him in the process. If the man in your life doesn't share your interest in art or antiques, find a friend who does.

On the face of it, you might think that spending more time with your friends takes away from your relationship. But I believe it can actually add to it. First off, if your friends are their real selves and own up to their own imperfect unions, you'll quickly realize you're not the only one whose husband thinks a distracted nod counts as paying attention. Listening to someone else gripe about their husband usually puts my own into a more positive light. Or at least reminds me that they're all like that.

This is all easy for me to say because I've got a good one. I hope you do too, but if not, you might need some of that friend perspective even more. They'll listen to your "he just doesn't get it" woes and chime in with a few of their own. But let that leapfrog into, "he drinks too much" or "he won't let me sign off on the checking account" and you're going to get a different kind of support.

A few friends outside the relationship can take some of the

pressure off the people inside it. Whether you need them to help you over the rough spots, share your favorite hobby, or remind you that the insurance policy doesn't pay off if you murder him, they're cheaper than a therapist and they're almost always on your side.

Having said that, if you really want to be happier in your relationship, some actual time together is probably a requirement. I doubt bill-paying and home improvement projects do much to keep the romance alive. Sometimes even a vacation doesn't do the trick.

I just came back from a vacation with my family that was anything but. If you've got little kids you know exactly what I'm talking about. It's hard enough to manage them in a controlled environment, but to do it with an ocean and uncovered electrical outlets nearby makes a paying job look easy.

I came home more tired than when I left. I was also less than pleased with my significant other. It seems he went into the vacation thinking it would be a chance for rest and relaxation. Unfortunately so did I. We spent most of the trip annoyed with each other because we weren't getting a chance to do it. And to think, we paid hard-earned money for this experience.

My friend Shannon, a marriage veteran with three little kids tells me, "Your problem is you keep thinking these 'family things' are going to be fun for everyone. The problem isn't him, it's you. Quit expecting him to be excited about hauling a diaper bag and port-a-crib everywhere you go. Get a baby-sitter and get over it."

If you don't think your man is fun or romantic enough, you need to ask yourself what kind of an environment he's forced to operate in. If every situation you're in together is about negotiating who does what, I doubt it creates much merriment for either of you. Sure you deserve more help around the house, more respect, and lavish gifts on all-important occasions. But you also deserve more fun in your life.

Don't let his lack of cleaning capabilities or gemstone surprises keep you from having it. Trust me, it takes years of intensive training to get a man to ante up on those. But most men can deliver on the fun part pretty easily. Remember, they don't have that running to-do list in their heads that keeps them from enjoying things. On the one hand, it's hugely annoying that you're the only one that keeps up with it, but on the other hand, if there's ever somebody that would be excited to see you drop it for a while it's your spouse.

Most of the men I know are more than eager to do something not task- or kid-oriented with their wives, they just need a little help to get the ball rolling. Sure you'll have to arrange for the sitter, but if you tell the man in your life you'd like to have some fun together, he can probably come up with something. Don't get too picky. Visions of Mr. Perfect whisking you away to Paris will only set him up for failure. Be nice and try to reciprocate.

I hate to be a nag here, but women aren't the only ones that are a little disappointed in the difference between courtship and cohabitation. Remember those 264 extra thoughts men are so distracted by every day? We might have gone into it with dreams of wine and roses, but they actually went into it thinking it would mean more sex. Guess we weren't the only ones that didn't have a clue what this game was about. I've asked around and the biggest complaint most men have about their marriages is not enough sex.

The normal female response is usually along the lines of, "Well I might have a little more energy for what's on *his* list, if he would help me out a little with *mine*." It's pretty pathetic, but sometimes sex can seem like one more responsibility, one more person who wants something from you. If that rings true for you, try to remember, we're going for better, not perfect. And in my eyes better means sharing your life with someone inspired enough to show up for it.

Let me put it to you another way: If you were having a morale problem with an employee and all you had to do to keep them motivated was to spend fifteen to twenty minutes with them a few times a week engaging in what I hope is not entirely unpleasurable activity for you, you would do it in a heartbeat. You want more fun, romance, and a better attitude from the man in your life? This is a sure-fire way to get it.

My own dear husband has chosen to speak out on behalf of his entire gender when he says, "Most men won't admit it, but we're really simple creatures. If we don't get enough sex it clouds our brains and we can't remember to do anything else." At least they know it. Now if you can't stand the person you're married to the last thing I want you to do is prostitute yourself

just to get some extra help around the house. But if you love
the guy, keep in mind just how motivational your personal
powers of persuasion can be.

Which brings me to an even harsher reality of love over the
long haul. No matter how romantic he was at the beginning,
it's a rare breed indeed that doesn't lose some steam as he goes
along. I don't know if he wooed you with wine, flowers, poetry,
or just opening the car door. But whatever it was, I'm guessing
you're probably experiencing less of it than you used to.

Before you jump to the conclusion that less of that means
he thinks less of you, take a look at what else he's doing. Earning
a living, bathing the kids, and keeping the oil changed in your
car might not feel like romance. But if they're making your life
better maybe they are. Hearts and flowers play well at the beginning, but somebody who shows up for the tough stuff is
worth keeping until the end.

So there it is—"motivational" sex, a date every now and
again, and some good friends to see you over the rough spots.
It may not sound like the happily ever after you had in mind,
but they'll help you keep it together until you get there.

Everybody doesn't ride off into the sunset with Prince
Charming. And if Mr. Perfect exists he's already married to Ms.
Perfect and they're out there somewhere driving everyone
around them absolutely insane. Accepting your man for who
he is doesn't mean you're settling for less. It means you've got
the good sense to enjoy the best of what he has to offer.

Cinderella's story ended while she was still young and beau-

HAT DID YOU EXPECT?

tiful and could fit her foot in a glass shoe. I'm thinking you had a little bit longer tale in mind.

WHY DIDN'T YOU SAY SO?

I can tell I really made a difference when:

A. Someone names their first child after me because I have shown them the true meaning of life.

B. I am showered with compliments, flowers, and jewels.

C. My contributions are spotlighted in the latest issue of *Miracle Worker* magazine.

D. I can see it for myself.

When we complain about all we're doing for everyone else, we're usually more frustrated by the lack of appreciation than by the work itself. In a perfect world everybody would see the things you do and provide heartfelt gratitude at every opportunity. Because we've already established that we don't live in a picture-perfect world, I doubt you're experiencing thanks as much as you would like.

Anyone who feels like they're spending their life cooking, cleaning, and chauffuering knows all about this one. Nothing is more frustrating than fixing a meal or cleaning up after someone only to have it go completely unnoticed. Or even worse, being told you're doing it incorrectly.

Or maybe it's a paying job where you're feeling taken for granted. How many times have you slaved away on a project and then not heard a bit of feedback on it? I can think of numerous instances where I jumped through hoops making someone else's deadline only to have it sit on their desk for two weeks. It's hard to feel like your work is really valued if you think it's going into a black hole.

Sometimes, we eventually resent activities we actually volunteered for. You know, that stuff that we *should* do out of the goodness of our hearts. At least this stuff ought to matter to somebody.

My friend Margaret was hoping to make a difference when she volunteered to be the coach for her daughter's soccer team. She had played soccer herself and while she didn't make a career of it, she did remember it was fun,

> *"I really enjoyed it as a kid so when my six-year-old came home from school saying she wanted to play, I thought, great. It wasn't like there were tryouts or anything, we just signed up. I think she was more excited about the uniform than anything else.*
>
> *Nobody else volunteered to be the coach, so I said I'd do it. I knew the rules and I thought I could make it fun for the girls. They were only in first grade. I figured, how hard could it be?"*

Coaching the girls wasn't hard, it was the parents who were a nightmare. Every time Margaret turned around one of them was complaining about this or that. Their daughter wanted to play a different position, they didn't get the schedule on time, no one told them when they were supposed to bring the snack, their child's uniform wasn't right, practice ran late, and on and on and on. There were ten girls and every single parent had something to say about how Margaret was running the team. It was bad enough that no one thanked her, but when they started to criticize her it was just too much. As she says,

> *"The sourpuss looks were the most annoying. Anytime I took their daughter off the field they would just glare at me. I wasn't even playing my own kid half the time just so I could get everyone else's in. Didn't these people realize I'm just a volunteer mom and I'm doing the best I can?"*

You know why people don't appreciate the things you do? They're too busy trying to get their own stuff done. Whether they're trying to be a good parent by looking out for their kids or are just too wrapped up in their own brains to look up, they're more concerned about their own agenda than they are yours.

It's depressing but true; something usually only registers on their radar screen when it's not working the way they think it should. But let's be honest here, haven't you ever been guilty of the same thing? Do you send a note to your child's teacher to tell her what a good job she's doing or to find out why his paper got such a bad grade? Do you show up at your neighborhood meeting to thank the people that care enough to keep things going or to complain about the trash pick up? Do you tell your boss how much you're enjoying your coworkers or complain about how they can never get anything done? Do you thank your baby-sitter for being on time or complain when she's late? Do you tell your spouse you're glad he took out the trash or grumble when he doesn't?

There's absolutely nothing wrong with bringing problems to someone's attention, you'd never get anything fixed if you didn't. I doubt any of us have the time to thank people for every little thing. But when all you hear is the bad stuff, it's easy to lose sight of the good stuff. Margaret's team actually got a lot better as the season went on. And even more importantly the girls had a great time. Which was exactly the reason Margaret chose to do it in the first place.

FLASH

It still makes a difference, even if they don't say thank you.

Maybe they're not appreciating you the way they should, but maybe they're not getting any positive feedback in their own lives either. People aren't undervaluing your contribution, they're just worried about their own. When you're ten items behind on your to-do list, you tend to forget everyone else has one as well. Especially if they make it look easy.

It has been my personal experience that if you do something

well and with a smile on your face, people think it took no effort whatsoever. Margaret was always her nice, positive self at practice so it never dawned on anyone that she might be having a hard time. Every time someone approached her with a suggestion she smiled and said, "OK, I'll do my best." How were these people to know she drove home, hands clenched on the steering wheel, swearing she was never going to do this again? But Margaret didn't want to stop coaching, she just wanted somebody to say thank-you.

If you don't want to quit what you're doing, maybe there's some way you can feel better about it. One thing you can do is to realize the difference between a request and a complaint. Those soccer parents simply wanted special attention for their own child. Asking for it didn't mean they thought Margaret was doing a bad job. It just meant they had their own agenda. The next time you hear some version of "what about me" take it for what it is—somebody thinking about their own hide, not going after yours.

If you do run across somebody that seems to have it in for you, don't take it to heart. They may just be having a bad day and you were the first ready target they came across or maybe they just never stopped to consider your point of view. If that's the case, go ahead and share it with them. But keep it nice. If you fire back with, "I can't believe you're complaining about this when I'm blah, blah, blah . . ." it's going to have the opposite effect of what you're trying to convey. Try something like, "Oh gosh, I'll really try to work on that. I'm feeling so overwhelmed by everything I have to do, that it's hard to keep it all straight, but thanks for letting me know about this." Trust me, the guilt factor will kick in enough to at least get them to be quiet. They may even offer to pitch in.

If you're feeling a little bit testy you might try doing what my brother does. When he hears a complaint about his work he often responds with "It sounds like you're really interested in this, I guess I can count on you to handle this one in the future." You can just imagine how many suggestions he's been offered after that response.

But what about those jobs where no one even notices what you're doing. If I had to pick anything, I would say that domestic duties rank at the very top of the list when it comes to unappreciated work. Every woman I know feels like she does more than her fair share and it goes completely unnoticed.

One thing you have to realize is that your family's not intentionally shoving it off on you; they don't even know it needs to be done. You can't thank a person for something you're blissfully unaware of. Remember how people don't speak up unless there's a problem? Well, the better you are at this job, the less they realize you're even doing it.

I don't know about you, but one of my biggest frustrations with my own family is that I have to be the keeper of the list. They may handle a few items, but I'm still the one that has to create it. You know what I mean. That list of who needs to be where when, what so and so needs for their such and such, the pick ups, the drops offs, the baby-sitters, and gifts for every occasion, including some you don't even attend.

I'm here to tell you, I've been in some high-pressure jobs and this scheduling and tracking is harder. The mental brain-power it takes to coordinate the school, work, sports, and hobby calendars of one family is enough to drain an Einstein. Try to do it in a less than filthy environment with enough nutritional meals to keep them from keeling over and you have the recipe for a meltdown.

Given all the effort we put forth, you'd think the incentive plan would include trophies, trips, and checks. But noooo, the payback for doing this job well is that they keep adding to it. Competency is rewarded by more opportunities to display it. The least they could do is throw you a bone and tell you how much they appreciate it.

But they don't. At least not as often as we think they should. And the reality is they probably never will. To make matters worse, the people that are closest to you are usually the worst offenders. Whether it's your family assuming the clean clothes just show up in the drawers or your boss thinking that elves sneak in at night to run all those reports, when you consistently do a great job for people they're more likely to take you for granted. Or perhaps they do appreciate it, they just neglect to tell you.

Have you ever had the delightful experience of hearing that someone you're close to said something very nice about you to someone else? Like the time you found out your boss told his boss he "never could have pulled it off without you." Or maybe you overheard one of your kids say, "my mom comes to all my games, she loves it." Even something as simple as finding out your parents said how proud they were of you can move us to tears.

One of the high points of my own marriage was the evening I got a new perspective on what my husband really thinks of my contributions. We were at his annual company party, he had changed departments that year and I was meeting some of his coworkers for the first time. As I chatted with one woman, I was shocked to find out how much she knew about me, our kids, my work and, this was the real kicker, "what a great job I do of keeping our family organized." My first thought was, "I can't believe it, he has gone and gotten himself another wife. I'm just like those clueless women on television who find out their husband has another family on the side." Surely he hadn't been talking about *me*? Was this the same man that rolled his eyes and groaned every time I forgot to pick up the dry cleaning?

Once I remembered he has neither the time, energy, or money to become a bigamist, I realized that, yes, he was talking about me and had a very high opinion indeed. Granted, I loved hearing it from this woman, but where had all this positive reinforcement been hiding for the last few years? I asked him about it on the way home.

He couldn't believe how surprised I was by her comments. "I've said that to you before, and beside it's so obvious why would you ever question it?" I guess that keeper of the list job wasn't going as unnoticed as I thought. Truth be told my husband does compliment me, not as often or as eloquently as I would like, but he occasionally says something nice. I just have trouble hearing it and believing it when it's sandwiched between a couple of screaming kids and a request for more timely laundry. If you don't feel like you're getting enough appreciation or feedback, ask yourself if you might be disregarding some of it.

Sure it feels more validating when they praise your efforts to someone else, because then you know they really meant it. They weren't trying to cheer you up on a bad day, they didn't want something from you, it wasn't mixed in with a bunch of negatives, and you didn't have to solicit it. I have to tell you though, if you insist on discounting any praise that doesn't come to you exactly the way you want, there's not going to be a whole lot left over.

FLASH
Compliments still count if you have to ask for them.

Compliments aren't going to spring forth every time you need one, so you might as well get over it. The better you are at your job the less likely they're going to consider you even need any praise. After all, someone as good as you *should* be able to observe the obvious. The reality is if you really want positive feedback, sometimes you're going to have to ask. Just

because you requested it, don't let it diminish the response.
However, be careful here, I want this strategy to work for you not against you.

That same sweet husband and I almost came to blows on the Disney World monorail when I tried to solicit a little feedback. It was summertime and my youngest child was about six months old. We went to visit relatives down near Orlando and for some unfathomable reason I thought it would be a good idea to spend a day in the park.

Some of you more experienced mothers are probably quite correctly questioning my sanity at this point. What kind of nut takes an infant to an amusement park in the height of the tourist season? And in Florida no less? My only defense is that we were in the area anyway and I was still under the influence of post-baby hormones. So off we went.

I packed a stroller full of gear, left early, and was hell-bent on having a good time. The minute we got into the park I snagged a map and scoped out our day. I was still nursing, so I had to plan around the best times to be at the kiddie rides for our older child and a quiet place for me and the younger one at three-hour intervals. It was hot and sweaty and the lines were so long you forgot what ride they were for.

It wasn't all misery. Our five-year-old enjoyed herself, I found a place to nurse, and the baby napped in the stroller at the appropriate times. All due to my great planning. At the end of the day, as we rode the monorail back to our car, I decided I deserved some positive reinforcement, so I turned to my husband and said, "You know, it wasn't easy to pull this off, but I think I organized it well. The older one had a great time, I kept the baby on her schedule, and I even got us out in time to miss the traffic. Don't you think I did a great job?"

His response was something along the line of, "I've lugged a ton of stuff around this godforsaken place, spun around on those damn teacups so many times I think I'm going to throw up, and I'm hot as hell. If you're fishing for a compliment from me, you can forget it."

I told you earlier kids, bosses, and husbands need special handling. Remember the I'm up, you're down seesaw? If they're having a hard time too, it becomes an absolute roller coaster. In his defense, I like to think I would have gotten a better response if I had asked earlier in the day or even waited until it was all over and the kids were asleep. I've learned that if you really want someone to tell you what they think of your work, wait for a time when they can understand the question.

That's not to say that you should put it off indefinitely. If you wait until you're so resentful you're about to burst, you probably won't ask very nicely and even if they do respond, I doubt you'll believe the answer. If you have to clench your teeth to keep from screaming your request, you've probably let it go too far.

Just because they let you know what's not working, it doesn't mean they think everything is bad. We can come out of a glowing performance review, but if there's one thing that needs improvement it's all we focus on. It probably has something to do with the fact that it's the only thing that requires any action on our part. That, and because they're usually not so descriptive on the good stuff. "Keep up the great work," is pretty easy to ignore because it just means more of the same.

If you're having trouble remembering the positive information, try asking for it a little differently. The key isn't more compliments; it's more meaningful ones. People intuitively know how to describe the effect you have on them or their organization when the feedback is negative. If they think you're not up to par in a certain area, they want you to know the impact of it so you'll be motivated to fix it. But most people don't possess the same skills when it comes to handing out praise. They assume "great job" says it all. It takes a little prodding to get them to describe the consequences of positive actions.

The next time someone tells you whatever you did was "just great," tell them it would mean a lot for you to know *why* it was so wonderful and what *effect* it had on them or whoever else you did it for. Maybe they hadn't thought about it in those terms or maybe they didn't understand how important it is to communicate the positive consequences. Either way, a more descriptive answer usually leaves both parties more satisfied with the exchange. Feedback on how perfectly it matches the picture is easy to forget. Understanding how it mattered to somebody is much more memorable.

When you think of what you do in terms of the impact it has on people, it helps you focus on the good parts and filter out all the bad stuff along the way. And the clearer *you* are on how much it matters, the easier it is to accept when other people are too busy to notice.

I hope you'll use some of these suggestions to make yourself feel a little more appreciated for whatever you do. And if you can't see it for yourself, you've got my permission to ask for some reminders. Everybody deserves to know what they're doing counts for something.

If you really want to make a difference, I'll let you in on a little secret. Go back and reread this section thinking about how you can use these ideas to make somebody else feel better rather than just applying them to yourself. There's probably a soccer coach in your life that will be glad you did.

Perfect is when everyone tells you how much your work means to them. Better is when you can see it for yourself.

THAT GIRL

When I was younger I dreamed that one day I would:

A. Lead a whirlwind life surrounded by beautiful people all enamored of me, the most beautiful one of all.

B. Be lauded by saints and sinners alike for the contributions I have made to better humanity.

C. Become rich and famous making everyone that was ever mean to me pea-green with envy.

D. Forget about everybody's else's standards and create some 229
of my own.

WHAT DID YOU EXPECT?

I was at the doctor the other day and as usual the nurse started the exam by weighing me. Despite removing my shoes, belt, and earrings there was no refuting the concrete evidence. I weighed exactly the same as I had the year before. And this was the year I had vowed to lose the extra weight I had been carrying around since the birth of my second child.

Hey, it wasn't like I hadn't tried. I changed my diet and I'd nearly exercised myself to death doing aerobics, weight training, and everything else that's supposed to melt the pounds away. But quite frankly, I was completely disappointed by the results. Those size six jeans were closer to fitting the toddler than they were me.

As I brooded about my weight, the nurse proceeded to take my pulse and blood pressure. When she was done she turned to me and asked, "Do you exercise very often?" "Yes, I do," I replied, but before I could go on about how it obviously wasn't working. She said, "I can tell. You have a really low heart rate and your blood pressure looks great."

I'm embarrassed to admit this, but until that moment I thought the entire purpose of working out was to look better.

⚡

FLASH

It's not about your looks, it's about your health.

Once you get to a certain age, your looks might still be really important to you, but your health is what's going to last.

Yet, here I was so worried about the size of my waistline that I had completely ignored the fact that I had gotten myself into decent shape. You'd think I would have noticed that I no longer huffed up the stairs. But no, I was too worried about how wide I looked in the mirror on the landing at the top. Now that I thought of it, I actually felt better than I had in years.

When all you're concerned with is how it looks, it's easy to forget how it feels. Our bodies aren't the only place we make this mistake. We've got just as exacting standards for everything else. Every time things don't look like we think they *should*, we miss the good part. I kept picturing that dream body in my mind and anything else was cause for misery. I was comparing myself to someone else's picture when I would have been better off creating my own.

Those impossible standards you insist on measuring yourself against weren't created in your head, the rest of the world came up with that perfect picture. If you feel like your life isn't meeting your expectations, ask yourself where they came from. Are they based on some fantasy you concocted when you were too young to know any better? Or some version of perfect you bought into along the way? Either way, it's time to move on. The girl that came up with those images didn't have all the information. She only knew what she thought it was supposed to look like, she forgot to think about how she wanted it to feel.

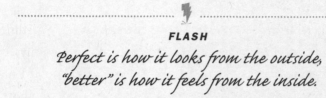

FLASH

Perfect is how it looks from the outside, "better" is how it feels from the inside.

The more time and energy you waste presenting your fake self, the easier it is to lose sight of your real self. The perfect picture is based on what everybody else thinks. It's time to figure out what you think.

What is it you want in your life? Is it happiness, love, joy, appreciation, or some fun? You'll never find it if you stay wrapped up in outside appearance and images. Once you start looking inside, I bet you'll discover what you're looking for in the life you've already got.

Finding happiness in the life you have isn't about how well it matches the picture or even what other people might think about it. It's about how you feel about it. Maybe you didn't become a prima ballerina; maybe you're doing something better. Maybe you're doing something with your time that matters to somebody.

You deserve better than running around in circles trying to make your life look like the perfect picture. You deserve some time to think about what's important in the big picture.

CHAPTER SEVEN

What Time Is It?

"You can have it all, you just can't have it all at once."

—A 1973 Harvard MBA, twenty-five years older and
wiser than when she first took on the world

IT WORKED FOR SCARLETT

One of every woman's biggest problems is time. There's never enough. Try as I might I am still haunted by the *should list*. As a child of the '70s I simply *assumed* I would have it all, so my personal *should list* is quite daunting.

Then came the first baby, and as every mother knows, that changed everything. Before she was born I assumed I would take a three-month maternity leave, find good childcare and go back to work, continuing to conquer the universe. It had certainly been done before.

My mother's death just before my daughter was born gave me quite a wake-up call, so I was pretty open to the idea of rewriting my script. But I had committed to be back at work in three months and I had bills to pay, so I really didn't feel like I had much choice.

The week before I went back to work I mustered up the energy and organizational skills to hire a baby-sitter and take myself to the hairdresser. My roots had gotten to the point where it looked like I was going for some sort of punk rock effect. If I was going to reenter the work force fat and still wearing maternity clothes, the least I could do for myself and anyone that looked at me was to have decent hair.

As I sat under the dryer waiting for the bleach to work it's wonders, I picked up a magazine. Thumbing through it, I happened to glance down at an article about Sandra Day O'Connor. The old me would have loved reading something about a successful powerful woman like that, after all I was planning on just as stellar a future for myself. The new me almost didn't look at it, because for a fat woman in sweatpants who measures her life in the two-hour increments between nursings it was just too depressing. But smiling Sandy in her judge's robes must have still had some appeal to me, so read it I did.

I can't even remember what the gist of the article was; all I remember was that while reading it I had another flash. As the writer described the honorable Judge O'Connor's brilliant career, I realized that when she was my age, she was a housewife!

It was in that instant that I realized a life can be long and there was a lot of mine ahead of me. I was thirty and my daughter was an infant. If I got off the fast track for ten years, I would still have twenty-five years left to work. That was more than three times as long as I'd already put in. All of a sudden I was free. I didn't have to do it all now. One of the other problems with my *should* list wasn't just what was on it, but my assumption that it all had to be done simultaneously.

I had been looking at my life in terms of the grand plan, each thing that I did was built on the last thing and I had to continue heading down the path I was on. I suddenly realized that instead of looking at it in terms of what I had to get done by certain tick marks, I should look at it as what it was—a life, not a business plan. I didn't have to plan everything now.

FLASH

Deciding what to do now isn't deciding what you will do with the rest of your life.

In the immortal words of Scarlett O'Hara, "Tomorrow is another day." The decisions you make today may affect tomorrow, but you don't have to script it all now. I am finally realizing that I have permission to change my mind.

A mother's death does a lot of things for and to a daughter. One of the things losing our mothers did for JoAnn and me was to make us realize that we will both eventually die. If someone had asked before I lost my mother "Do you think you'll die one day?" of course I would have said, "Yes, everyone dies eventually." But I thought that was going to happen to some old lady that was in no way connected to who I am now. Once it happened to my mother I realized that it wasn't going to be just some old lady, it was going to be *me*, and maybe it wasn't going to be at one hundred like I planned. I might be fifty-three.

I never had the chance to ask my mother about the life plan she had for herself when she was younger. I knew her well enough to know she probably had one. After all that's what us hard workers do isn't it? Make a plan. Without knowing the details, one thing I am 100 percent certain of, it didn't include dying at fifty-three.

Your life can be long or it can be a lot shorter than you planned for. The question is, what are you going to do with it, or rather with the rest of it? Because no matter how old you are at this very moment that's what you have—the rest of it.

That day under the dryer thinking about the rest of my life, I started to use *frontsight*. My friend Rachelle, the Good Samaritan who is tirelessly improving the healthcare of the ladies in the nursing home, said to me once, "People don't regret the things they do, they regret the things they don't do."

On the face of it, this might make you feel even more like you have to do everything, but as you think about it more, I think you'll see what she meant was, that people regret missing a window of time—a time they can never get back.

As I talk to some of the *wise women* I've met, what strikes me is that when they talk about the choices they made or didn't make; they have the advantage of hindsight. More than just knowing how things would turn out, they also know what proved to be important and what ended up not mattering at all. They aren't caught up in the details of the moment so they can see it clearly.

Foresight is the ability to look ahead and hindsight is the ability to look back. I define *frontsight* as the ability to jump ahead and look back in advance. It's really simple: leave the problems of the moment and imagine you're in the future.

Imagine you're ninety years old sitting on your front porch looking back over your life and you're focusing on where you are right now. Now you can see what the most important things in your life are. What are they? As you look back at that younger woman you are now, what are you going to wish she had done with this window of time?

You remember Suzanne, the great sales manager who loves helping her people. During a business dinner she told me that she had the chance to take a promotion with her company and move to Europe. It was a wonderful opportunity, a three to five year stint in London with travel all around the rest of Europe on the company dime. Suzanne is single, forty-five years old and has no children, so there wasn't any reason not to go.

When she told me about it, I thought, "Wow, I hope I have the chance do something like that one day." Clearly this was an opportunity of a lifetime and she wouldn't want to miss it. I thought the answer was obvious, but I asked her anyway— When she looked back years from now what would she wish she had done, stayed in Dallas or gone to England? She thought about it for a while and said,

"You know I'm really happy here. I've spent a lot of time developing a great group of friends. I see my nieces and nephews all the time and it means a lot to them and me. Plus, you know my parents are older and I don't want to miss this time with them. If I go out of the country for five years, my nieces and nephews will grow up, I'll lose my friends, and my parents will get even older. The job would be so demanding, I doubt I would be able to come back much, so you know, I guess I want to stay right here. I can always go to England on a vacation if it's that important to me. I've got the rest of my life to see Europe, but I want to enjoy the happiness I have now."

I'm sure everyone thought she was crazy, but she made the right choice for her. Suzanne's answer demonstrates what the chance of a lifetime really means. It isn't always the opportunities that are presented to you, it may be something or someone that's right beside you every day.

FLASH

Our lives are a series of windows that open and close. The hard part is figuring out which ones will close forever.

It doesn't matter how old we are, there are always some open windows. Just ask the lady at the garage sale.

One thing I should have already told you about JoAnn—

she describes herself as incredibly cheap. I prefer to think of her as frugal. One of the ways she saves money is by scouring garage sales in fancy neighborhoods. She was at one of these bargain hunter's delights about to fight a woman for a nice camelback sofa when the woman's daughter came up to them. The daughter told the woman she shouldn't be buying the sofa because she was probably going to be moving soon. It seems the daughter wanted the mother to move from her current home in Birmingham to live with her in Atlanta. The woman looked to be about seventy and the daughter wasn't comfortable with her mother living two and a half hours away. The woman told JoAnn that she wasn't so sure it was a good idea, she was doing fine where she was. But then maybe her daughter had a point. Although her health was good, anything could happen.

Clearly she had a decision to make. Since we have no trouble jumping into the lives of strangers and they are surprisingly receptive, JoAnn told her, "You're only going to have this time once. Twenty years from now how are you going to wish you spent it?" The woman immediately answered,

"Doing what I'm doing right now spending time with my friends, my church, my clubs and driving to see my daughter whenever I want to. I've got such an active social life where I live. If I were to move in with my daughter I would give all that up and I just realized I would never have it again. Never! My daughter works all day so I would be alone. I can always move over here if I need

to, but now might be my last chance to have this great social life."

Something tells me there was a little mother-daughter chat later that day.

I shared the windows-of-time idea with another friend, Nancy, a consultant I've worked with now and again, who gave the most surprising answer yet. We were talking on the phone one day about an upcoming project and she said,

> *"I have this great opportunity to take my business in a whole other direction. It really appeals to me, but things are going well now so I'm not sure if I should change."*

By this point, I had used the *frontsight* technique on a few other friends and was getting downright cocky about my ability to help people figure things out. Knowing that I would be able to get her to take advantage of this great opportunity, I confidently said to her, "You have a window that's been opened to you. Ten years from now what are you going to wish you'd done with it, something new and exciting, or the same thing you'd always done?" She replied,

> *"You're right, I do have a window and this makes me realize I should be spending more time with my horse."*

> *"I just love jumping in shows. I'm thirty-five years old and I don't
> see anyone on my circuit over fifty. I've got to spend the next
> couple years getting my horse in shape so that we have some
> really good years together jumping."*

So much for my insights as a career counselor. It made total
sense once she explained that the horse circuit and her friends
there were the great loves of her life. This just proves that if you
want someone else to give you the right answer for you they
can't. They can give you an opinion, but like mine with Nancy,
it's based on their idea of your windows, not the grand passions
in your life that you know you don't want to miss.

At first when JoAnn and I came up with *frontsight* as a way
to identify your windows we saw it as a technique for making
the big choices. But we found it works for the little ones as well.
In fact, it makes you realize just how little they are.

The other day JoAnn was all in a dither over a situation with
her son. It seems he was dating a young woman she thought he
was getting fairly serious about. She had some reservations
about whether or not she was the right girl for him. (She has
yet to admit what we all know; no one is ever going to be good
enough.) One of the things she was concerned about with this
girl were her unrealistic career expectations. She was deciding

on a career based on what she thought she would be paid without knowing what the job actually entailed.

JoAnn's big dilemma was, how serious was he about this girl? Was she going to be her future daughter-in-law? If so, JoAnn had better pitch in and help the girl figure out her career plans. Should she arrange for her to view her future profession up close and buy her some books on the subject, the way she had her son? Or should she tactfully let her son know she thought he could do better? Or could he? Was the girl just young and hadn't had much help or was this a major character flaw? What to do, help, not help, butt in, butt out?

She imagined she was ninety and looking back at herself right now. What would she wish she had done? The answer was obvious—help her. If she turned out to be her daughter-in-law, she would have gotten to know her better and ultimately made life better for her son by helping his wife's career. If they broke up, then JoAnn would have spent time helping a young woman who needed it. In the end it was not a big deal and she couldn't believe she had spent time worrying about it.

Oh sure, she gets the easy ones. Her child is already raised. But what was I going to do? When I began this section talking about time and my own daunting *should list* I realized I was going to have to give something up, I was just trying to decide what.

It came down to this: Work was a long window and being with this amazing daughter I'd brought into the world was a short one. Once I saw that clearly, I made my plans.

Choosing how to spend your time doesn't always mean giving things up, it just means deciding.

Up until that point in time, I thought work meant seventy hours a week, fully charged, all engines running, a life-consuming endeavor. It defined me, it's what I was. To give it up would mean I had wasted all that time building my career.

But that was the old me. My mother had died, I'd had a child and suddenly the world looked a little different to me. I realized my choice wasn't giving anything up, it was *choosing* how to spend my time. If I chose to spend it differently this year than last year, it didn't mean how I'd spent it the last several years had been a waste. I'd enjoyed it and I'd made a good living.

I *decided* that because quitting altogether wasn't really a feasible option, I would just have to change the way I worked. The fact that my company was a mess and I hated my new boss so much I couldn't see straight greatly assisted me in my decision-making process. I worked part-time and eventually, quite shamelessly, stole some of my company's customers to go to work for myself.

I still work and I still like it, but it no longer defines me. I'm trying to make the most of my window of time with my children and trying to earn a living in the process. I have days where one suffers at the expense of the other, I just try to keep remembering which window is going to close in ten years and which one still has thirty to go.

If you think I'm going to leap from here to that mothers shouldn't work full-time, I'm not. I only told you my story so you'd know how I came up with this stuff and that I try to practice it myself. If you happen to be facing that particular dilemma yourself right now, I don't envy you. The choice I made was right for me. But, I hasten to add, I do not have your child, marriage, checkbook, or career.

Remember, we dumped the *should list* several chapters ago. Once you've done that you can go about making yourself feel better about the life you're already living and more confident about the life you have yet to live. You can actually make your life easier by setting some things aside. There are some windows that can wait.

I was talking with my friend Jennie, the gorgeous one who discovered some real friends when she got cancer and divorced. We were both lamenting our lack of effort on civic affairs. My mother got a nature trail established, so I should do something right? I'm a proud PTA parent and participate in all the other mommy activities, but I've always had this nagging sense of guilt that I don't do something big.

Once I used *frontsight* to look at my windows, I realized that my window for community service is basically open until the end of my life. If I manage my finances right, and can actually retire, I could spend an entire decade from sixty to seventy

devoting myself selflessly to ridding the world of evil and disease
and creating harmony among people. My God, with ten years
there's nothing I couldn't do!

Jennie's first comment was, "What a relief, I am totally off
the hook on that one. I mean I can just put that aside for now
and not feel guilty about it."

She's right. I was already putting it aside, but I had been
feeling guilty about it, a wasted emotion if there ever was one.
Once again I was free, I'd get to it, I just wasn't going to do it
now. Besides, if I listened to my own advice I would know that
raising two little girls is quite enough contribution to the world
for now.

There are probably a lot of things in your life that you have
to do. Sometimes it doesn't matter what window is closing, you
still have to take out the trash, do the laundry, make a living,
or whatever. But you can put the demand list out of your mind
for just five minutes. Trust me, no one will handle it while
you're not looking.

Imagine that you're ninety years old and you're looking back
over your life. At that point you won't be worried about the
details of things, you'll be thinking about what really mattered
to you at the end of the day. Your kids are grown, there are no
more jobs or promotions, and you probably don't even get invited to too many parties anymore. You're sitting in that rock-
ing chair looking back at the woman you are right now. I don't
know how old she is, thirty, forty, fifty, or even sixty, but she
looks so young to you. What do you want to tell that younger

woman? She's sitting right next to you on that porch and she wants to know: What really mattered in her life? She's got a lot of years ahead of her, what will she wished she'd done with them? What chance of a lifetime does she have right in front of her, right now, that's going to go away forever one day?

Is it older parents, a great business idea, a baby to rock, a sick friend to comfort, a husband to romance, a teenager to straighten out, grandchildren to spoil, a grown child that needs some help, a community in danger of a developer, or even a horse to ride?

What are the windows in her life that she can go back to and which are the ones that are closing? How do you want her to spend this time? From where you're sitting, the answers are pretty clear. Take her hand and tell her. And tell her why. You can see how much pressure she's under, so if she can get back to it, give her permission to put it aside without a moment's guilt. If a window is closing, tell her to make the most of it right now. You know she won't regret it for a minute.

It's not just about where you spend your time; it's about where you spend your heart. Ticking off items on the *should list* won't make you happy, it just makes you tired. Save your efforts for what really counts.

I'VE GOT A FEELING ABOUT THIS

When I'm faced with a really big decision I:

A. Get my tarot cards and deal 'em out.

B. Look around to see if there isn't somebody else that can play the grown-up for a while.

C. Go ahead and supersize it.

D. Listen to my inner voice because it's got a long history of steering me in the right direction.

It's not always easy to figure out which windows are closing. If you're me, one of the windows I consistently neglect is my window for fun. I usually can't get around to cracking it, much less make the most of it.

Yet I was determined to have some fun last year, so I ordered tickets to one of those concert series where you buy a package of tickets for several different performances. We weren't big fans of all the artists, but what the heck? Any concert's more fun than the laundry and bill paying we have been doing on the weekends.

Wouldn't you know it? The morning of the first concert some friends called us up to say they were having an impromptu party that night and could we please come. The scheduled performer that evening wasn't one of the more popular artists, so selling the tickets was not an option. But this was a party with friends we hadn't seen for quite some time. Given our flimsy social life we hated to turn it down.

We had already paid for the tickets, so we decided the best we could do was to swing by the party on the way. "No problem," they said, "just come for as long as you can, it's last minute and really casual." We went and just as we were starting to have a good time, we had to leave. As I explained to our friends, "We would really love to stay, but we already had these concert tickets, so we have to go."

Just as we were about to walk out, one of our friends commented, "You know you really don't have to go. You've already spent the money, now it's just a question of how you want to spend your time." He was right, we didn't want to go to that concert, we wanted to be with our friends. It wasn't a waste of money to stay, it was a waste of an opportunity to leave. We took off our coats and had one of the most enjoyable evenings we'd had in a while.

There are some pretty obvious crossroads in our lives where one part of your life is over and another is about to start, like having a child, finishing an education, or deciding which job to take.

But there's a whole lot of other decisions we make every day without even realizing it. Keeping your job, staying in a relationship, living where you do, or sticking with your original Saturday night plan. Those decisions might not seem like watershed events, but the sum of these choices is what constitutes your life.

The best criteria for making them is figuring out what you really *want* to do. I was talking to my friend Ellen the other day and she said, "I've hung on to this cold for the last two weeks and I'm just not enjoying my life." My initial reaction was, "Oh right, I forgot, I was supposed to be enjoying it." Sometimes in the grand scheme of things that's pretty easy to forget.

If your life isn't everything you want it to be and my suggestions haven't made you feel any better about it, maybe it's time to rethink your plan. If there isn't enough fun, excitement, love, challenge, or rest in your life, it doesn't have to stay that way.

FLASH

Just going through the motions is a decision.

Once we've invested a little time or money in something, we assume we have to keep going down the same path. Heaven forbid I let my concert tickets go to waste. I was willing to give up a great evening just because I'd already paid for something else.

If you've started off with one direction, you don't have to continue. The last thing you deserve is to get yourself so busy you can't even recognize when it might be time to change course. I had an excellent boss once tell me,

"The mistake most big executives make is they don't allow themselves enough brainstorming time. When they're coming up the ladder they have more time to think, but as they become more successful, their time is scheduled down to the minute. It's a

shame because that kind of thinking is probably what got them to the top in the first place."

The same holds true with anything else. Unless you take some time away from it, you're never going to be able to figure out what to do about it. How can you decide if your job is working out for you if you're expending all your brainpower doing it? I'm here to tell you it's a lot easier to mull over what kind of mother you want to be if you don't have a bunch of kids screaming in the background. You can't get a clear perspective when you're inside a situation.

If you don't like the script you were handed, check and see who wrote it. Even if it was you, give yourself permission to do a rewrite. If you don't like the show, you can just walk out of the theater. Even a gambler knows when to hold 'em and when to fold 'em. Just because you stop doesn't mean you're a quitter. It means you have the good sense to know when it's time to reevaluate.

I don't know what kinds of choices you're facing in your life. Maybe it's something new that's come your way. Or maybe you're deciding whether or not you're happy with things just the way they are. Whatever you're facing, know that decisions don't always present themselves in little A, B, or C packages. If they did, it would be a lot easier to recognize when it's time to make one.

We need to give ourselves time to do the thinking.

I'm not talking mountain-top meditation here, sometimes something as simple as a bubble bath will do. All you want to do is give yourself some time to forget about everybody else's agenda and figure out your own. The rest of the world put all those items on your *should list*. It's time to re-create it as a *could* list so you're the one who can choose what goes on it. You could do this or you could do that, *should* doesn't have to weigh anywhere in the equation.

If you're having trouble thinking it out, there's a part of your brain that will be happy to tell you what to do, but you're going to have to take the time to listen to it.

Intuition has been called the sum of all our other senses. We've all got it, it's just a question of how much we trust it. Yet, how can our senses collaborate if we insist on keeping them otherwise occupied twenty-four hours a day? I can multitask with the best of them, but I have never once had a flash of insight when I was talking on the phone, making the dinner, and watching the kids at the same time. It's pretty hard to get clear on your thoughts, when you're so busy reacting to everything else going on around you.

Going with your gut doesn't come naturally to everyone. My friend Shannon says her intuition is like, "a good friend, if you snub it for too long it will quit talking to you." If you're having trouble getting in touch with yours, see if a few of these techniques help you find it.

One tried-and-true method is to put two columns on a sheet of paper with the pluses on one side and the minuses on the other. Remember, the key here isn't the length of each column, but how you *feel* about it. Some of the best decisions I've ever made had a long list of reasons on the minus side and a simple "because I want to" on the plus side. Adding another child to our family is an example that most immediately springs to mind.

Perhaps you're the kind of person that likes to talk things out. I know the brain is supposed to work before we talk, but mine doesn't *start* working until my mouth has already been at it for a full five minutes. This isn't the greatest technique for a presentation, but it's helped me figure out more than one dilemma. Trying to articulate it for someone else forces me to get clearer on it myself.

Another thing that's helped me get a better perspective on things is to imagine what I would tell someone else to do if they were living in my life. Suppose a friend, relative, or a stranger on an airplane asked you what to do. What would you tell them? All you mothers out there might want to think about how you'd like your child to handle things if they were in your shoes. You might not think they ever will be, but if they are, your example has already told them how to act.

It's up to you to figure out how you can make the best decisions; I just want you to recognize which ones are yours to make. I've already asked you to think about what your windows are and what's going to be really important to you at the end of your life. Now I'm asking you to listen to your answer. I can assure you, you're the only one that's got it.

You know that little voice in your head that's always reminding you how you don't measure up? It's time you told it to shut up. It may sound like it belongs to you but it doesn't.

Once you've silenced it, you can start listening to the one whose opinion matters a lot more. That's yours. You know what you want to be doing with your life. You deserve to start doing it.

THIS ONE'S A KEEPER

One of the things I've noticed about women is that we're always saving it. All the stuff that's somehow not good enough for our regular old lives and must be saved for a special occasion, like our best outfit, nice perfume, decent towels, or our real jewelry—the good stuff.

With JoAnn, it was candles. For years she has enjoyed nice candles. Well, at least she enjoyed buying them or getting them as gifts. They were, of course, too good to use every day, so she saved them. In fact, she had an entire box filled with various types of wonderfully scented candles she was saving for a special occasion. The queen never did come over for dinner, so that box of candles is still in JoAnn's garage. Only I'm not sure you could call them candles now; unscented, discolored, melted, misshapen blobs of wax might be a more accurate description. The few that still have their wicks may come in handy one night, but unless you call a power outage a special occasion, most of them are long past their heyday.

It's not just company we try to save things for. Sometimes it's for ourselves. My friend Jodie tells me that she has a whole drawer full of lingerie she hasn't worn in years. "Well," she says, "I guess I'm always thinking that we'll go off on a romantic weekend sometime and I'll wear it then. That and I'll lose ten pounds before we go." Jodie and her husband have two little kids, so they don't get to those cute little bed-and-breakfasts too often. And as far as how she looks goes? Well in my personal experience, it doesn't usually take a negligee to get a man interested, but if she's waiting for that weekend to feel romantic herself, all I can say is Valentine's Day is only once a year. Besides, in my book, if my husband and I ever go to bed at the same time, with the same level of energy, in the same, shall we say, mood . . . it *is* a special occasion!

As for me, I used to be particularly obsessive about my best perfume. At least I was until a birthday I had a few years back. It was Labor Day weekend and my husband and I had, appropriately enough, spent the day working in the yard. Our neighbors were having a cookout that night, which was just as well, because having spent our money on azaleas, we were too broke to go out for my birthday.

It was a casual get-together, but I showered and put on clean shorts before we went over. I finished dressing and was deciding whether or not to use my good perfume. The previous Christmas my husband had given me what I considered to be *expensive* perfume. It probably cost at least $50.00 a bottle, and it was definitely in the saving-it-for-a-special-occasion category as far as I was concerned. The drugstore knockoff was for every day.

So there I was, going to my neighbor's party, on my birthday, debating whether or not to use it, when all of a sudden it dawned on me—my life doesn't get any better than this!

It's bad enough I didn't think I was worthy of decent perfume on a daily basis, but if I wasn't going to use it on my birthday, when was I?

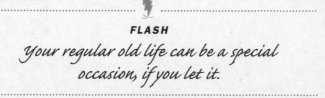

FLASH
Your regular old life can be a special occasion, if you let it.

You can go through your life as beautifully or as sloppily as you choose. Just don't go through it waiting. Waiting for this part to be over and the good part to start. Waiting for when you finally:

Get a new house, don't have to buy diapers, make more money, lose twenty pounds, retire, get married, tell your boss to take a hike, go on vacation, have a baby, get a dream job, become a grandmother, move, finish your novel, or whatever.

Those things might happen and your life might be better when they do. But do you really want to wait until then to start enjoying it? There are a lot of things that are worth more if you save them for later, but your happiness isn't one of them. Plan for the future all you want, but don't make the mistake of putting your life on hold until it gets here.

So spray on the good stuff, hug the kids, forget perfect, and start living it. This one really is it.

I began this book talking about my mother, so I think I'll end it the same way. In a lot of ways this book was a tribute to her and to the life she led. But it was more than that; it was about the life I wish she'd led.

The things a mother does every day are an example for her children, especially her daughters. My mother set some pretty high standards that I've tried my best to emulate. She also did some things I've been determined to handle differently in my own life. But one of the biggest lessons I learned wasn't from watching my mother live, it was from watching her die.

Dying from cancer isn't pretty, as anyone who's seen it will tell you, but there is one consolation; you usually have *time*. If there's any stuff between you and the people you love, there's time to clear it up. As with most mothers and daughters, we certainly had some stuff. But it's amazing how all that goes away when you know it's about to end.

I recently read an interview with a doctor who had been with a lot of people on their deathbeds, and he talked about what their last thoughts were. His comment was, "in the end, it's all about who you loved and who loved you." He was right.

I was there for my mother when she died. There the way everyone deserves to have someone there for them. There to tell how much she meant to me and how much I loved her. There to tell I knew how much she had done for our family and to thank her. There to hold her hand and tell her not to worry about a thing. I would take care of it.

My mother died a peaceful death, knowing that she was loved and appreciated by the people that mattered. I only wish she could have spent more of her life that way.

It shouldn't take dying or having someone you love die for us to see that. Sure, I wish that I could have said it better before she got sick. I wish a lot of people could have. But more than that, I wish that she could have seen it for herself. We shouldn't have to wait for some deathbed testimonial or an eloquent eulogy to finally feel like we count. It's there every day, just waiting for us to see it.

When our friends brighten up at the sound of our voices, when our neighbor looks to us for a sympathetic ear, when our husband wants to know why we're late, when the teacher calls us for the decorations again, when our coworkers share a laugh and some gossip with us, when our parents still tell us what to do, when all the kids always mess up *our* houses, and even when people sometimes take us for granted are the ways people tell us we matter, that we're important to them. It may not be the way we want to hear it, but they're saying it. And if you've made her day a little brighter and the mother at the checkout looks a little less embarrassed over her screaming kid, she's saying it too.

My mother's life counted. It counted for a lot, and if she didn't know it while she was alive, I hope she does now.

You know what? So does mine and so does yours. And if you don't believe me, just ask the lady at Wal-Mart.

BIBLIOGRAPHY

Books

Anderson, Peggy. *Great Quotes from Great Women*. Lombard: Celebrating Excellence, 1992.

Covey, Stephen R. *7 Habits of Highly Effective People*. New York: Simon and Schuster, 1989.

Elium, Jeanne and Don Elium. *Raising a Daughter*. Berkeley: Celestial Arts, 1994.

Ford, Betty. *Betty, a Glad Awakening*. Garden City: Doubleday & Company, Inc., 1989.

Keirsey, David and Marilyn Bates. *Please Understand Me*. Del Mar: Prometheus Nemesis Book Company, 1984.

Popcorn, Faith and Lys Marigold. *16 Trends to Future Fit Your Life, Your Work, and Your Business*. New York: HarperCollins Publishers, Inc. 1994.

Tannen, Deborah. *You Just Don't Understand: Men and Women in Conversation*. New York: William Morrow and Company, 1990.

Tieger, Paul D. and Barbara Barron-Tieger. *Do What You Are*. New York: Little, Brown and Company, 1992.

Yancey, Phillip. *The Jesus I Never Knew*. Grand Rapids: Zondervan, 1995.

Articles

Morris, Betsy. "Tales of the Trailblazers: Fortune Revisits Harvard's

Women MBAs of 1973". *Fortune.* v 138 no. 7 (Oct. 21 '98) pages 106–8.

Reyes, Sock. "Consumer Reports on Health." *Consumer Reports*, v 12 Issue 3 (March 2000) page 2.

Other Materials

Vital Learning Corporation, *Customer Oriented Selling*, Omaha: 1990.

Lisa Earle McLeod is a working wife and mother. *Forget Perfect* is her first book. Her life includes a husband of fifteen years, two little girls, a huge mortgage, a job, and laundry piled high in the foyer. Her greatest passion is making a difference to women and trying to improve this crazy world before her two daughters have to go out into it.

Lisa's pre-writer past includes stints as a salesperson, executive coach, marketing consultant, sales trainer, and PTA officer. She currently works as a writer and speaker, lecturing nationally to corporations, parent groups, and educational organizations. She has a degree in journalism from the University of Georgia. Lisa and her husband, Bob, live outside Atlanta, Georgia, with their daughters, Elizabeth and Alex.

JoAnn Swan Neely, is a wise—not to be confused with older—woman who has faced numerous domestic hurdles during her thirty-two-plus years of marriage to the same man. Her most significant accomplishment to date is a college-educated, multitalented, community-active grown-up she is proud to call her son. She is currently president of her own healthcare consulting company. She and her husband, John, live in Atlanta where their biggest hobby is helping their son, Mark, remodel his first home.